FIRESIDE MISCELLANY

A Collection of Irish Memories, Meanderings and History

Printed and bound in 2018 by
.brand printing company
www.bws.com.ua

Published by Denis O Higgins
dohiggins49@eircom.net

ISBN: 9790988377219

© Copyright Denis O Higgins, 2018.

All rights reserved. No part of this publication may be reproduced or used in any manner whatsoever without the express written permission of the publisher except for the use of brief quotations in a book review of scholarly journal. Enquiries concerning reproduction outside those terms should be sent to the publishers seeking permission. Except in the case of historical fact any similarity to persons who may have existed is merely coincidental.

While every effort has been made to ensure the accuracy of all information contained in this book, neither the author nor printer accepts liability for any errors or omission.

© Cover photos by Bróna Higgins
Front cover: "Tossey's Cottage" in South Armagh
Back cover: Walking in the Mourne Mountains

Content

Our Farm and Townlands............................8
The Kicking Cow of Moneymore......................10
Rural Electrification – A Fight against the Light............12
Folk of the Shannon...............................15
On the Bog.......................................18
The Burning of Knockcroghery (June 1921)
and its All-Ireland Connection 21
How Much for the Eggs Paddy?......................23
Counting Sheep...................................25
The Lone Peddler.................................27
Pigs In Flight...................................29
Our White Cow Whinger............................31
The Little Brown Hen.............................35
I Met Her at the Maple Ball......................37
The Old Homestead................................40
Back to School...................................43
Sean South and Mulligan's Safe house.............47
Foiling the Border Smugglers.....................49
Papal visit to Ireland 1979......................51
The Auld Lammas Fair.............................53
No Pub, No Pawnbroker, No Police:
Bessbrook' Quaker Code...........................55
Widows' Row......................................57
The Newcastle Fishermen..........................59
The Yelverton Affair.............................61
'Uncle Jack' The Jovial Gent of Glaslough........63
Letterfrack's Dark 'De'formatory.................66
The Cahan's Presbyterian Exodus 68
Cultra's Hand and Pen Orange Hall................71

Dan White's Dander 73
Victoria Crosses. 75
1916 Fatal Ship Collision at Carlingford Lough 78
General Robert Ross. 81
China's Great Wall. 84
Free Travel Pass. 86
Limerick You're a Lady. 87
A Treat in Rostrevor. 89

(By Josephine)

McDonald's Of Glencoe 92
A Doll of Grace 94
Better Late And Alive. 96
Flora McDonald 98
Monastic Settlements of Rostrevor 101
Finvola, the Gem of the Roe 104
Paris and it's Pere Lachaise Cemetery. 106
Oscar Wilde and his County Monaghan Connection 108

Foreword

In this book, Denis O Higgins shows us his gift of being able to write stories that are snapshots in time. From his youth on a farm and right through his adult life, his eye is a camera giving us photographic stills of a rapidly changing Irish countryside that in many cases has faded in the rear view mirror of modern life.

'Fireside Miscellany' as a collection of these stories is almost an anachronistic label now as people prefer to sit watching boxes in the corner of their living rooms.

Yet it was around the kitchen hearth where the art of story-telling was perfected in rural Ireland to keep alive tales and people of times past.

I strongly commend these stories for the way they too build a bridge for our future generations about how their forbears lived in the past.

By sharing stories of his past, Denis transports us to the farming days of yesteryear using humour, love, realism and honesty. An engaging and compelling collection of short stories

PJ Cunningham, author of The Long Acre (Short-listed for Irish book of the Year 2014).

Introduction

Denis was born into a large family on a threadbare holding in the west of Ireland. As an elder sibling, he, at the age of nine, had to forgo his childhood overnight, when following his father's untimely death at age forty five, he was called upon to shoulder the added share of never-ending farm-work. In later years his professional work took him to settle in Monaghan, where he now lives, in retirement, with his wife Josephine (nee Mc Donald) and daughter Bróna, whenever she makes the occasional return from her exploits overseas.

Many of these stories are drawn from the experience of growing up on a small, stubborn and indebted farm in the 1950's and 60's. That bygone era was a time when all farm work was completed manually and the use of horse and cart was then the closest that the farm came to mechanisation.

Josephine (nee Mc Donald) is a native of Monaghan. She also grew up on a small farm in this less progressive period. Her voice is occasionally heard on RTE Radio's Sunday Miscellany programme when reading her selected chosen stories.

One inclusion in this book, "I met her at the Maple Ball" relates the initial then-fairytale meeting of Josephine and Denis at the Maple Ballroom at Rockcorry, Co. Monaghan.

Other writings flow from the experiences and reminiscings from family camping days, which took them all over Ireland and included the occasional sojourn abroad to Scotland and France .

They rarely pass an old graveyard without inspecting it's headstones and recording some of the many interesting scripts. They often find that the ingredients for unique stories are found hidden in such repositories of history and silent resting places.

Acknowledgements

I wish to extend my warmest thanks to my wife Josephine (née McDonald) and daughter Bróna, for their story contributions, encouragement and their time and patience in editing and finalising the project. Thanks also to Bróna for the photographs that now adorn the covers of this book.

My sincere thanks also to the esteemed author PJ Cunningham, Ballpoint Press, for his advice and his gracious foreward. Writer Lorna Sixsmith was likewise most generous in her guidance, for which she deserves high praise. Ann Crilly of the library in Newcasle, Co. Down was also very helpful in providing me with research material. Likewise, Mary in the Linenhall Library, Belfast, was also quick to assist when approached.

To the characters of my youth that have endured in my memory and imagination throughout my life, and who now populate the daydreams of these pages, thanks for the everlasting impressions and images. For those who have passed on, may they rest in peace, and for those still living may you prosper in peace. *Go n-éirí an bóthar libh.*

To all those along the journey who helped in any way, I extend a big *"go raibh míle maith agaibh."*

Our Farm and Townlands

While most countries have their electoral divisions, Ireland is globally unique for being divided into townlands which total just over 60,000. In most cases, where the original Gaelic name still remains, its usage rolls off the tongue like honey in June. The very mention of such ancient names enables the listener to form a mental picture as to its size, elevation and the topography of the related unit of land. This is because our townlands usually derive their names directly from their natural definition. Irish people have shown themselves to be proud of their unique heritage. Back in the troubled 1980s, when an all-out official attempt was made in the Northern counties to dispense of these divisions in favour of postal codes, the retention of the townland names was the sole issue that brought all sections of the differing communities in campaigning together on its behalf. Sadly the change was eventually imposed on all counties, with the exception of a 'stubborn' Co Fermanagh. Similarly, Government attempts to downgrade townland addresses in the south of Ireland, are being largely ignored by the rural residents who refuse to engage with the new official codes.

I grew up in a townland called Moneymore. Unfortunately the reality was that it did not live up to its apparently affluent connotations. The name Moneymore is anglicised from its original Gaelic of *Muine Mór* meaning 'The Big Shrubbery'. Unfortunately that shrubbery did exist - we owned most of it – and it covered a huge portion of our 40 acre arid farm. This wasteland, while an ideal wildlife habitat, did not contribute to farming profits. Not content with only a townland division, our farm was further sectioned by allocating an individual name to each of our twelve fields. This task must have been carried out with scientific zeal as the 'white field' acquired its name because it grew an abundant crop of white dog-daises each spring. Similarly the 'long field' happened to be much longer than its width. The 'last field' was positioned at the furthest away point from our dwelling while the 'new field' was the most recent addition to our holding.

It was only as a result of much research that I found out why our 'Mc Connells field' was so named. Even though that family name did not exist in living memory there, I established that a gentleman bearing that name did reside nearby on his small farm over a hundred years ago, and therefore our adjacent field will forever preserve the memory of the long departed Mr. Mc Connell .

Our local area had an alternative name as it was sometimes referred to as 'The Racecourse' and this was even used and officially accepted as the postal address used by some neighbouring residents. This title was derived from the ancient and long defunct three mile horse racing course which still envelopes many local farms and dwellings, including ours. Despite being redundant for over a century its flat surface and clay embankments still remain intact.

That facility, to accommodate 'The Sport of Kings', had been installed by the local Crofton landlord of nearby Mote Park Demesne. No doubt many a wager was won and lost on its grassy banks by members of the former ruling class.

No such fanciful notions or leisurely pursuits endured through the years for my family in our shrubbery-filled plot, however.

A major and enduring problem was the lack of domestic and farm water, particularly in summertime. Our farm was void of waterways or springs and the local communal bore hole was years away. The heavy metal spouting, which channelled the welcome rain water from the dwelling roof into the big concrete tank, was always maintained in good order, awaiting the rainy day. The wooden barrel, which stood to attention beside the cow shed, was always in position and at the ready to catch the run-off from its tin roof.

Despite this careful collection and storage it was still necessary to devote much valuable time in the dry months to the slow and tedious task of ferrying water with the horse and cart, from the river, back the three miles to our thirsty cattle and sheep.

Very little food or material went to waste in our full house, and this imperative often applied whenever a goose or chicken was killed for dinner. One of my youthful stunts was to gather up the feathers and entrails of the unfortunate kill and pack them neatly into a cardboard box. The package was then covered in brown paper and tied with twine, similar to that parcelled by a then shopkeeper. I set my trap by leaving the completed product at the edge of the public road, with an invisible fishing line attached, which I then threaded in through the hedge. In time an unsuspecting cyclist would stop, look around and try to lift his fortunate find, probably believing that an earlier cyclist had unwittingly lost their purchase. Just as the sly hand came in contact to lift the package, while hunkered out of sight in the foliage, I would tug the line rapidly in order to pull the parcel from their reach. With shock and disbelief the red faced bounty hunter would re-mount and peddle away at speed.

After a few rounds and tiring of my game, I would replace the parcel on the road and from a hidden distance watch as some unfortunate passer-by lifted the parcel and hurried away with the prize tucked under his arm. Unfortunately I would miss the gory official opening when the duped punter would arrive home and set about unwrapping to check the contents of their find. I could only imagine the extent of their annoyance, embarrassment and disappointment.

The Kicking Cow of Moneymore

Each morning the same traditional itinerary guided the daily farming chores. It was my task to go to the fields and coax all of our seven cows into the byre, secure the chain around each animal's neck and place a dish of meal at each head. Then return to the dwelling and have a quick cup of tea before I began the milking process. One mild September morning, when I went to gather our herd, the big whitehead cow was missing. While her absence was unusual I tended to the others and then set out through the farm to find her. She was a bit of a rogue, so I expected to find that she somehow made her way into the neighbours land. However on first inspection I failed to locate this wanderer. I returned to the byre and milked each of my now-impatient animals and released them back to the outdoors.

Now I had time and urgency to find my lost animal. First I scanned the 'high field', then the 'white meadow'. Next was the 'long field', then to the new paddock and finally to the last field. On failing to find her I commenced to search through our difficult, ten acre terrain, covered with briers, tall trees and clinging whins but still without success.

While making my way homeward, through the 'top field', I thought I heard a mournful muffled sound. I followed in that direction and peering into the deep ditch, I found my missing cow. She was lying on her back and seemed to be in a distressed state. It appeared to me that she had laid too near the open dyke, and somehow rolled into its deep hollow.

When word spread, the neighbours started to gather with their shovels, spades and sturdy ropes. After removing a wide patch of earth, the ropes were tied around the cow and, on the count of three, all the willing men began to pull. In time, they succeeded in rolling the rescuee into the new opening and propping her into her normal resting position.

I thanked the men as they departed, all well satisfied that they had concluded a great feat. However, when she refused to respond to our tasty food offerings and quiet coaxing, the vet was sent for. He arrived and gave her his best attention, including powerful injections. Contrary to our expectation, her condition failed to improve, so I made her last days as comfortable as possible before she faded away. Her loss was huge, both as a beloved animal and as a valuable asset.

The word went out that we needed a replacement to ensure our continuous supply of milk. Some days later a well known cattle dealer called to our home, with a fine white-head milking cow. She looked the ideal replacement so after a long discussion of 'splitting the difference', the agreed price was paid over to the dealer and the sale was only finalised when he handed me back a fiver as the 'luck penny'.

We housed our new cow and pampered her with hay, water and meal mixed with kind words. That evening when I placed the metal bucket in place and hunkered down to milk her, she flicked her stinging wiry tail across my face and before I could recover she made a wide-sweeping kick and knocked both me and bucket flying against the barn wall. I made allowances for the bovine as her surroundings were strange and the milker new to her. However when I tried again I received the exact same touchy welcome.

Even though events were becoming frightening and dangerous, I still had to complete my task as to leave her un-milked overnight would leave the animal in severe discomfort and could also lead her into health problems. The only option was to tie a weighty stone to her kicking "device" and immobilise that leg until milking was complete. Much as I disliked restricting her in this manner, I tried this new form of management by wrapping a rope round a stone block - that I could barely move myself - into position, and attaching the other end around the bovine's back 'kicking leg'. I then sat down and re-positioned the bucket and myself and started to milk again. Now, she unveiled another stealth tactic by promptly lying down, almost trapping me underneath in the process. The last resort was to tie the unfortunate back legs together, on a very short rope. Now each time she attempted to kick the bucket; she had to struggle to remain standing.

This savage manoeuvrer had to be completed morning and evening during each milking time. Nevertheless, I found this an ordeal, and even the thought of it made each milking a feared chore. Clearly the cow had some painful or nervous disposition when it came to milking. Getting the vet to attend to the problem was out of the question as that would cost money, which was in very short supply.

Despite being fed and watered carefully, the engendering hardship took its toll on the poor animal and eventually she 'went down' and refused to get back on her feet. After some difficult months of sickness she died. Her huge financial loss was mourned, yet secretly I breathed a sigh of relief as the daily task of trepidation had at last come to an end.

Rural Electrification – A Fight against the Light

It was back in the black and white days of the late fifties, when rural life moved at snail's pace and little changed or improved. Life merely rotated from one season to the next. Each new month dictated the mundane manual work programme on the cluster of small uneconomic holdings in our locality. Now and then the talk was of the new energy source called electricity that was supposedly sweeping across parts of Ireland, in areas that we and our neighbours had only heard of, and weren't even sure existed at all.

Some argued that the electricity, if it ever arrived to us, would be carried on poles placed along the public road and could present a danger. Wiser, more travelled voices, confirmed that the ESB poles would be erected on farmland to carry the new power from one dwelling to the next. Nevertheless, most householders in our locality were suspicious or indifferent to this scheme as they didn't value the need for this unknown service or its intrusion into their quiet lives. A local rumour had it that this electricity could travel in a straight line only, so many residents who dwelt off the beaten track didn't even bother to enter the connection debate. However, the greatest drawback was that it's introduction would create an additional bill which few families could afford to pay.

The local debate was short lived by the immediate arrival of the gangs of robust men who were noticed walking through the fields with their maps and markers. They rarely bothered to establish the name of the land owner or ask permission prior to entering or surveying private property. It was different times and the ESB personnel came armed with the knowledge that despite the mutterings of local disapproval, the affected farm owners would not dare question any actions flowing from an 'official body'.

One aspect which caused great concern was the positioning of the ESB poles, many of which could have been located beside a fence or a natural boundary, but were instead placed some distance away from fences thereby spoiling many fields. This action seemed to facilitate ease of work for those manoeuvring the poles into place, with little thought toward the farmer or protecting the integrity of the land.

I was attending the local National School at the time, and because the distance was shorter by field than by road, I usually walked the near cut through the fields to school. It was a great novelty to watch the gangs do their digging, which resulted in a very deep hole being excavated, and then, with all their strength and many shouts, the men manoeuvred the huge pole into an upright position. Some of their roars were directed at me and my fellow scholars, so as to ensure that we kept a safe distance away.

It was late on a Friday evening when the ESB ganger hammered a hazel stick into the hallowed soil of our front lawn. This marker was the usual signal indicating, to the installation crew, where the next pole must be erected. My mother was furious as, if embedded at the marked location, the pole would spoil her precious lawn and this new monstrosity, along with the additional cables, would permanently spoil the view of, and from, our dwelling.

Our first plan was to talk with the ganger and appeal to his better nature but the word was that this official didn't have such a virtue. He was a man of few words, who remained aloof, except to lay down the ESB law in rigid terms. So rather than appeal for him to select an alternative site, and thereby draw attention to our discomfort, it was decided to avoid him and say nothing. After all, we had until the following Monday morning to frustrate his plans. There was always another way of skinning that cat and we had to find the means.

From early the following Saturday morning all siblings, small and big, were assembled and prepared for hours of hard manual labour. My mother had decided that a flower and shrub bed would be fashioned in the corner of our small lawn, where the threatening hazel stick now reigned. The first task was to find a new home for this wooden impostor. The hazel was exiled and hammered into place some 15 yards away in our adjacent field, while taking great care to keep it in line with the poles already erected on either side.

Now all hands were put to work carrying suitable stones until a two foot high semi-circle free-standing stone wall enclosed the corner of our lawn. The next task was to carry buckets of soil and manure until the selected area slowly filled up to the wall level. Lastly we transplanted flowers and a few gawky shrubs onto our new bed. With some final adjustments we gave our new creation a more mature and permanent appearance, for the purpose of camouflage.

As expected the ESB crew did arrive, early on the Monday morning, and all equipped with their working gear. I took great delight in spying, on them, from within the protection of our home. The group of six shuffled and futured about for some time; they seemed to sense that something was amiss, but failed to solve the puzzle. Eventually they began their normal digging and luckily at the spot we had chosen, as dictated by the translated marker. Within a short time the new pole was raised and secured into place.

Later, that evening when the ganger arrived on his routine inspection, I watched again from behind the protection of the curtain, as he shuffled over and back alongside our lawn perimeter while shaking his head and directing his occasional glance, of disapproval, in the direction of our dwelling. He eyed up the situation and his demeanour left no doubt that he wasn't fooled. The fact that the new pole had held the line seemed to satisfy him sufficiently to allow it to remain in its alternative spot. It transpired that despite the local opinion, the ESB ganger did after all have a reasonable side to him.

ଓଃ୫ଠ

Folk of the Shannon

"We'll go to the Shannon" said Josie Hannon,
"No fear" said Andy Weir. "Ah do" said Tom Shaloo.
"What's your hurry?" said Peter Murray.
"Where will we dine?" said Bertie O'Bryan,
"On the grass" they shouted from Ballyglass?

These 'characters' of my childhood have all passed on to their eternal reward and unfortunately have not been replaced. During my early years the locality I grew up in was teeming with a variety of people; ordinary farmers, housewives and a few codgers who were unique in that each had their own distinctive mannerism and attitude to life. That individual uniqueness is all but disappeared now and, sadly, unlikely to return. This local ditty, never recited within their earshot, summed the reality of some of my former notable neighbours.

The Lough Ree area of the River Shannon was only a 3 mile bicycle trip away from the homes of all of these characters. It was the nearest recreational area - a place to meet and to swim - in those innocent days when dwellings didn't enjoy the luxury of running water.

Josie Hannon, an unemployed cottier, never busted a gut in his willingness to find permanent work. While often found walking the roads, he had a word with everyone he met. Despite his permanent cash-flow problems he nevertheless edged his way through life as fulfilled and happy as a millionaire. Because of his wandering lifestyle, he had the news of the country and loved to be first to distribute his breaking knowledge to anyone who stopped to lend him an ear. Josie gave the impression, to his many listeners, that it was himself who actually created the news.

Andy Weir, tall with an austere appearance was a hard working family man. He toiled as a direct unskilled County Council employee on public road maintenance in the days of horse and cart. On my way to National School I often observed him, his broad peaked cap always off centre and pushing his trusty black Raleigh with his shovel and spade tied on with binder twine. On my return homeward he was still there, and in the meantime he had tabled a long distance of the roadway. His cutting spade - work ensured that the water drained off the cracked surface from the yet-untarred roadway. *Andy* sometimes used his horse and cart to draw broken stones and shovelled the load along the road to fill the constantly growing potholes. He worked diligently regardless of weather conditions and only stopped when it was necessary to shelter under a local tree or a convenient shed from the rain. He boiled tea water in his old blackened kettle on a fire of roadside twigs and ate his meal in the open, often seen sitting on a convenient wall. His week's work didn't end on Friday but included a half day on Saturday as well. This hardy weather-beaten gentleman seemed to expect only the minimum from life. His menial income tallied with his expectation and just about enabled him to provide for his wife and family.

Tom Shaloo, was not of our locality, but having spent many years in the army (at least that was his story), arrived one day seeking accommodation. He wanted to rent a house and while he was looking around for a suitable permanent residence a local farmer decided to help by offering him temporary use of a vacant house on his out farm.

Despite the fact that the former dwelling hadn't been lived in for some years, it remained in reasonable order. Tom set about cleaning up his temporary abode by sweeping it clean inside and out, but forgetting to inspect the chimney. When all was cleaned, and in order to make the dwelling cosy, Tom set about attempting to light a fire in its large open fireplace. After many failures he realised that the fire wouldn't take root as, due to dampness and through lack of use, it would require something substantial to assist combustion. Tom walked the half mile to his nearest neighbour and asked for advice and it arrived in the form of a taste of petrol in a small container. The benefactor then took up a pivotal position at his top story window and watched with expectation. For a long stint all was quiet, then a puff of swirling smoke appeared over the ancient chimney, another plume and then a burst of thick black bellowing dust followed, with an assortment of sticks, wool, feathers and years of nesting material which had been stuffed there by the jackdaws into the vacant chimney over the years. Within minutes the angry piercing flames appeared, not only through the chimney, but out from beneath the cracking slates as well. The fire had spread rapidly, engulfing the two-story dwelling, with smoke and flames exiting through the doorway and bellowing through the cracking windows. Later the would-be occupier was found wandering outside - he hadn't suffered directly but the trauma did engender a state of temporary shock. Tom Shaloo took to his bicycle after putting out the word that he was on his way to meet and compensate the house owner. He never arrived there and was not heard of again in our part. He disappeared from our townlands into the same shadows that he had originally emerged from.

Peter Murray was a quiet, solid and slightly overweight farmer. He, and his wife, were considered big farmers as their land ownership far exceeded that of their neighbouring farmers. Whereas the average size of holdings was around 40 acres, Peter owned three parcels which totalled 100 acres, and all of it in prime condition. He was often heard to utter his mantra that *"fair and easy goes far in a day"*, and he acted accordingly. Never rushing, he was seldom known to get excited, regardless of weather conditions or the mountain of manual work that had to be attended to. He was an expert horse-man and along with all his wants in farm accoutrements he always kept two large work horses. A vivid memory of Peter is of him sitting on the front of his huge wooden hay cart, a cigarette protruding from his mouth, resting his back on the load of hay while guiding his brace homeward from his out farm. As a child I would climb aboard the back of the cart to hitch a jaunt, but somehow Peter would spot me through the hay load and insist that I dismount. I was too young then to appreciate that his demands related to concerns for my safety and mistook his concern as a cranky spoil-sport.

Despite being extremely thrifty, he was amongst the first to acquire a television in the county and the first in our locality. The erection of the TV aerial on his roof was the talk of the townlands for weeks, in an area where life stood still. He and his wife were very generous in inviting neighbours to ramble for a few hours at night to watch the sole channel then - RTE - with them.

Cap wearing and friendly *Bertie O'Bryan,* while robust and small in stature was huge in farming knowledge. He owned and managed a pub in the village. He was also the local butcher, who killed his own animals from the substantial farm that he had amassed over the years. He was a man who loved his food and his discerning taste caused a problem, particularly when he helped out at the normal trashing events. While other hands ate whatever food was put before them, Bertie had to get his special order as he was pernickety with his diet.

The *Ballyglass* locality was noted for its beautiful lake teeming with fish and wildlife and an ideal place for an open air meeting. It was a haven for the sporty men who fished from one of the rickety reed-woven rafts, which were always freely available on that Lough. Its clean waters were a favourite treat for swimmers. On warm summer evenings many a picnic was enjoyed on its grassy banks. Years later when I visited to dip my toes in *Ballyglass* Lake, I couldn't believe my deflated eyes as barbed wire and a flock of sheep were now colonising the officially drained and dried-out basin where crystal water had once shimmered in the summer sunshine.

On the Bog

Working on the bog was similar to the myriad of other farming tasks, in that the turf harvesting had to be completed each year. Turf was the only fuel available to us for use as firing, to warm our old dwelling and for cooking our meals. This was especially true prior to the introduction of electricity, which did not arrive in our area until 1958. As youngsters this chore was a particularly difficult one as it required strength and stamina, spread over many lengthy hot days. In our case the nearest bog was five miles away from our home and therefore we had to make our plan of attack well in advance. The first errand was to haul our two wooden turf barrows in the ass-drawn cart to our turf bank. Once delivered, the barrows were deemed safe, thanks to the unwritten bog rule dictating that belongings were never stolen while left there. Property was sometimes temporarily moved or borrowed without permission by another cutter, but it was always returned when sought. The next task was to dig away the heather and scraw from the top of the fresh bank and deposit the spoil to fill the hollow left from where last year's turf had been extracted. When this 'bank cleaning' had been achieved to the depth that exposed the new turf, then the actual turf cutting could begin. As the cutting ritual was weather dependant, we would usually start in late April and continue into May. Turf has a mind of its own and if the opportunity does not arise to dry, early in the season, it will refuse to altogether, even under sunny conditions. It takes that special seasonal wind to win it.

Each morning, after the livestock was attended to, all three of us siblings would set off from home early on our bicycles, loaded with slane, spades and shovel. Food, water and a kettle, along with the vital box of matches, would also be loaded. On arrival at our workplace the first important task was to hide our bicycles in a sheltered place because exposure to the hot sun could have the effect of lifting some of the many repair patches and cause a flat tube. Such a puncture would leave the owner to struggle with a long five mile walk home. We had no watches or timepieces then, but if the wind was in our favour, the distinctive Angelus at 12 noon, pealing from Kilteevan Chapel, spelled out the time.

Working on the bog was tough and relentless. While the eldest sibling, who was also the strongest, took his place on the prepared bank with sharpened slain in hand, we wheelers got into position. As he cut each new sloppy sod he flicked it in one fluid movement, to the eager pair of hands who placed it quickly on his barrow, as he prepared to catch the next sod. Then the barrow, loaded with heavy soaking sods was wheeled off to empty the load some distance away and the contents spread on the waiting heathery ground. Meanwhile the second wheeler assumed his place, thus allowing the cutter to continue unabated. When the peal of that noon Angelus bell did reach our ears its sound was delightful as it heralded our tea-break. The black kettle was 'swung' over a fire of cipins and heather, and within minutes the boiling water was wetting a sweet round of tea. The bog creates a special ravenous appetite and working there renders all food consumed, mouthwatering.

But after a short rest, and before we became too comfortable, the work had to re-commence. While we found the bog difficult, the cuckoo seemed to delight in that quiet oasis and kept us company with its continuous welcoming summer call. The presence of the musical soaring skylark was another visitor who lightened our work.

The later Chapel bell, signalled 6pm and confirmed that it was time to gather up, reload our bicycles and cycle home to complete the variety of waiting farm chores. If the weather held, another three days work would allow completion of the difficult cutting. Then after a week of it lying in wait, it was time to start the rearing of the turf.

While this initial 'turning' procedure was tedious and hard on the back, it was not as rushed or intensive as wheeling the loaded barrows. After two long days of stooping and lifting, this aspect of the turf harvesting was complete. A further two weeks and the turf would be treated to another turning. While each sod would be much drier at this stage it would also be smaller, lighter and far easier to handle.

However, a bigger task awaited before completion could be claimed. This was the footing and clamping which raised most of the crop off the wet ground; allowing it dry faster. When all the new fuel was thoroughly dried it had to be drawn from the spreading area to the nearest bog road for carting home. This preparation procedure was usually undertaken with donkey and cart. The placid ass, when gently coaxed, would traverse the soft under-foot boggy conditions while a pony or horse would panic if used to draw a load across soft ground. On one occasion I unwittingly discovered this fact, but almost to my cost. In my hurry I decided that I would speed up the removal process by leading my pony, with its bigger cart attached, onto the soft ground. However, when I commenced to lead him, pulling his load road-ward, the animal bolted and almost sped into a nearby river. That experience taught me a very useful and lasting lesson.

In the early years we drew all of our four lorry-loads of turf home the five mile journey, by horse and cart. The first load was always deposited in the fuel shed of our local Ballymurry National School. The remainder of our crop was drawn home to the haggard where it was stacked and freed in position, to protect it against the winter weather. In later years we hired a local driver to use his lorry to ferry the turf home. While this hastened the operation, it did require that every sod had to be thrown by hand, to fill the lorry. Once home, all had to be manually removed again as there was no tipping mechanism on lorries then.

Having all our turf home and secured in the haggard, created a feeling of great satisfaction as no matter what difficulties the winter might throw our way, we now had an adequate fuel supply to keep our home fire burning for another year.

CR&O

The Burning of Knockcroghery (June 1921) and its All-Ireland Connection

'Knockcroghery is a village of Tan burned down but now they have rebuilt it and call it a town'.

During my school days this refrain was often uttered by the older generation and it related to the village, which supplied our education, groceries, places of worship and entertainment, and where we sold our farm produce. It was our world, but as children we seldom thought about the significance of that epithet or questioned Knockcroghery's history. Owing to a lack of substantial family finance, survival rather than history and remembrance was our priority then.

The spring of 1921 was the driest in living memory and the warm weather continued unabated throughout the months of April, May and June. In mid June a violent incident occurred in the village of Glasson, Co. Westmeath, located some four miles distance outside Athlone. The pompous Major, a Mr Somerville, who managed the army barracks in nearby Athlone, lived the idyllic life in that quiet hamlet of Glasson right on the banks of the River Shannon. However, in early June his peace was disturbed when a few rifle shots were discharged into his comfortable riverside home. Afterwards, a vicious rumour circulated that the IRA suspects who had challenged the military authorities by shooting at the Major, had escaped by boat across the Lough Ree waterway to a safe house in the Knockcroghery area of Co. Roscommon. While Knockcroghery was never known as a hot-bed of rebels, the then military policy was to apply retaliation, at random, on some community and the people and property of Knockcroghery were an unsuspecting and easy hit-and-run target for the soldiers. Under the cover of darkness on 20th June 1921 a complement of Black and Tans were ordered into three lorries and on exiting the main gate of the Victoria Barracks in Athlone, were directed to travel down the Roscommon road. As the diesels laboured along the roughly stoned highway, past the villages of Kiltoom, St Johns and Lecarrow, leaving a cloud of white dust from the arid stony road, the soldiers trained their loaded guns on anything, man or beast, that moved in the countryside.

At around 1 am on that longest night of 21st June 1921 the convoy of dread reached the outskirts of Knockcroghery village. Their first stop was at the isolated priest's house, but after many failed attempts to set the property alight, the attackers departed quickly in order to maintain their element of surprise. Moving on, the convoy cordoned off the village itself and the Tans entered the private dwellings

21

and ordered each family and occupant at gunpoint out onto the dark road while ensuring that the captives took nothing with them except the nightclothes they were wearing. Then, by torching the tender dry thatch the attackers destroyed each cosy home, one after the other. Subsequent press reports confirmed that the flames and smoke, resulting from that horrific fire, were even visible to residents living across the River Shannon in Co. Longford.

One Knockcroghery building which was exceptionally spared, was a public house and dwelling, when the owner, an impoverished widow rearing her young family, pleaded that the business was her only means of income and to local amazement she was delivered the only miracle of the night when the commander ordered his subordinates to leave her premises intact.

The next-door property of publican and general merchant, John S Murray, was also attacked when he and his wife and family, were ordered to the road at gunpoint. The youngest of the family, Jimmy, then a toddler in arms, was years later destined to grasp All-Ireland fame for his village and county. During the attack, the Murray home and property failed to catch fire, despite repeated attempts by the Black and Tans, as this, the only three-storied building in the village, was unique in having a slated roof. Their two-hour spree of military terror resulted in the village of Knockcroghery being razed to the ground, with the exception of three premises.

Included in the inferno was the home and factory of the famous clay pipe-manufacturing factory of PJ Curley, which up to then was one of the biggest employers in the West of Ireland for close to 250 years.

In 1923 after the Free State was founded, the British Government paid compensation to the victims making it possible for them to replace and upgrade their former homes and property. However the unique factory, which had given widespread employment to five generations through the manufacturing of clay pipes (known as dudeens), with the PJ Curley name imprinted on each shank, was destined to remain permanently closed. Happily some things have never changed, just as on 21 June 1921 the same four pubs remain serving the public today. One such bears the name 'The Widow Pats' in memory of the lady who preserved it from Tan destruction. The business of the late John S Murray also continues to flourish under the Murray ownership. Overhead an All Ireland football hangs from the premises ceiling – the same football as was played in the winning 1943 and 44 finals. The same Jimmy Murray, only a toddler during the 1921 event, was destined 20 years later to captain his County into more All-Irelands than any other and to win two consecutive All-Irelands, which still remain the only All-Irelands ever won for Roscommon, and for Knockcroghery.

How Much for the Eggs Paddy?

Saturday was a different type of day and varied from other mundane weekdays. Saturday was shop day, but most especially Saturday was egg day.

In the dull 1950s the production of eggs on our small farm was very cost effective, as our flock of two dozen free range hens were fed on potato mash, whatever they found on our back street, and scraps; particularly the left overs from the daily dinner. A few of the more impatient and cheekier hens would occasionally sneak into our kitchen at dinnertime and grab a morsel of food from the floor before making a hasty retreat. Sometimes their exit was sped with assistance from the nearest boot. The departing hen would often drop a goodbye parcel in the form of a moist souvenir on our stone floor in her haste to escape.

All eggs were carefully collected on a daily basis from their makeshift nest boxes and from rustic hides where the few stubborn hens insisted on laying out. Care was taken, by the collector, to ensure that a 'nest egg' was left in place to encourage the avian to retain her selected hide. On collection, each egg was individually wrapped in newspaper for its protection and all placed together in a basket. Come Friday the eggs had to be prepared for exchange the following day. Those without blemish were carefully placed in a basin while the remaining soiled eggs were set apart for cleaning. Applying bread soda with a damp cloth and rubbing away all foreign matter achieved this imperative.

The cleaning manoeuvrer was a tricky balancing act, as applying too much pressure would break the delicate shell and destroy the egg while a lack of adequate elbow grease would not achieve the required cleansing result. Because eggs were traded in multiples of half dozen the destruction of even one egg was warned against, by my supervising Mother, as it would have the costly effect of rendering the remaining five unsaleable.

Each Saturday, Paddy, who was more of a social service than a businessman, would cause a stir by his arrival in his large blue travelling shop-van. In those years there were very few cars going by on our road, and only the occasional van. My mother's first question to him was always *"how much are you giving for the eggs today Paddy"*. His stock reply would confirm that their value varied little, not more than an old halfpenny per dozen from week to week or month to month, inflation didn't exist then. On presentation, Paddy would routinely inspect the eggs for cleanliness to ensure none had a cracked shell and that none of the smaller pullet's eggs were sneaked in for inclusion in the count. He would also reject any eggs, evident as having been washed, as those wouldn't remain fresh for long enough.

As each of our few shopping items were ordered, Paddy would carefully place these goods in his cardboard box and tot up their total price. He would then subtract the value of our eggs from my mother's purchases, and record the overall transaction in duplicate.

At the end of each month the outstanding monetary balance would be paid to the appropriate party. In the summer months the balance was usually in our favour.

However, over the winter months Paddy was usually the recipient of cash payments as our hens took a sabbatical from their laying schedule due to the adverse affects from the reduction in daylight hours.

Sometimes the cash flow had to be stretched to allow the purchase of a 12st bag of white flour for bread baking. Paddy would extract the weighty bag through the back door of his van and hoisting it on to his broad shoulder, manoeuvrer it into our kitchen and by sliding it from his back, would deliver the heavy bag to the safety of our large wooden chest. The process usually proceeded smoothly but occasionally disaster would strike when, during its entry, the flour bag made contact with a sharp protruding nail causing the precious cloth to tear. The damage to the bag itself was as much concern as the subsequent loss of flour, because when torn the material could not then be fashioned into a badly needed bed sheet or pillowcase.

Occasionally one of our flock would go missing for some time, and despite a widespread manhunt, she and the whereabouts of her nest would escape detection. Later we would be rewarded by her proud return with a flock of tiny fluffy new chickens in tow.

Had the real potential of our laying hens been recognised in the hungry 1950s and 60s, a bigger flock and proper management of our free-rangers would have put more food on our table and earned us a small fortune. We could have been the wealthiest family in a poor neighbourhood.

Counting Sheep

Having read through her little book once again and whispered my stories about the turkey and the peacock, I was satisfied that little eyes had closed and she was gone to dreamland for the night. I stole out through the doorway and tiptoed down the dark stairway, taking care to avoid stepping on the creaky spots. I had almost reached the safety of the kitchen, and back to rejoin my card game, when I heard a little voice calling and ordering me back to remind me that I had missed out part of the story.

She was correct, I had indeed taken a chance by relating the short version, but now caught out, I had to return to her little nest and repeat, not one but the two full stories from start to finish.

Even when I had exhausted all my usual tricks the little smiling head continued to bob up, so in desperation, I suggested that she start counting sheep to ease her into sleep. I should have realised that she would have no idea of what I was talking about, because unlike me, my wee daughter was removed by one generation from farming. While counting those woolly animals always did the trick for me, as it still does to this day, there was no reason how she could understand or benefit.

Growing up on a mixed farm, counting the flock was a daily pleasant and important chore, because if one or more was found absent, it was advisable to start the search at an early stage. A missing sheep could be caught in briers or find itself in danger, lying helpless on its back, and in need of human assistance to release it from its quandary. Also, on the occasions when some of the more athletic of the flock decided to jump the fence into the neighbouring farm, the adventurers would need to be retrieved at the earliest opportunity lest they become lost or misbehave while at large.

The most vividly embedded memories are those of herding the flock in the wintertime, when the animals lost their inhibitions of closeness to human company. Their meek change of heart was ushered in by hunger and their need to be hand feed, as the growth in their normal diet of natural vegetation became dormant and later totally absent during the frosty months. The result was that on sight of a bag or rattle of a bucket the flock would crowd around, almost pushing their master off his feet, and making it very difficult to distribute the feed of corn into their long wooden trough. These 'hungry months' was the period when it was easier to lead the timid flock than to drive them. Each one of our 40 animals had their own unique personality and were distinguishable from each other. I could identify each member of our flock from any distance.

Early spring was an important time on our farm as that signalled the lambing season and therefore demanded additional care. The greatest seasonal change was the 'night watch' which entailed setting the alarm to arise during the night, dress in warm clothing, take the torch from its comfortable perch on the warm hob and test its beam, then walk into the dark frosty night. On reaching the field, where the sheep were enclosed for safety and convenience, I would switch on the lamp and slowly rotate its piercing beam towards the flock to bring each animal into focus.

Even at a distance, the reflection of each pair of eyes would confirm the presence of every animal, usually all resting in close proximity in the driest part of the field. When all were found present it was also necessary to carry out a closer inspection to establish if any new lambs had been born since my previous visit. New arrivals had to be carried by hand to the security of the farmyard shed while coaxing the mother to follow after her new born. Often twin lambs were involved, but when triplets were born this caused additional husbandry.

Black eye stood out from the crowd. She earned her name from the thin strip of black coloured wool, which circled both her eyes. She usually provided two sturdy lambs each spring but occasionally surprised by presenting triplets.

When counting for sleeping purposes I am standing in the 'high field'. I have opened the stunted iron gate from under the 'sheep-creep'. This ground level, purpose-built opening in the wall, had a restricted height - low enough to prevent all taller livestock from traversing through it. As I watch the flock, at first they bunch beside this gap and shunt around in an undecided and reluctant pose. Then somehow the leader, always the same sheep, pushes her way to the front and without hesitation dips her head and walks through the creep. I count as each animal follows lazily through, one by one from the 'high field' to the sheltered 'long field' where they will be contained for the night. This scene had a soothing effect similar to that of watching a stream of rippling water dancing its way through the land-scape, and begets the introduction of a deep, comfortable and contented sleep. My mind watches as the sheep head for the tall reek to feed on the hay that I have arranged around a tall sturdy pole, solidly anchored in the ground. This construction ensured that as the haystack is consumed and thereby undermined at ground level, the remaining fodder will slip gently downwards intact. Without that solid centrepiece, the stack would split and fall apart and bury the unsuspecting foraging animals beneath.

Now as I visualise the feeding flock enjoying the comfort and safety in their nightly surroundings, I also relax as I drift into a deep peaceful and contented sleep.

The Lone Peddler

I was about 5 years old the first time I noticed him. Just freed from National School for another day, I was running homeward with the other children like a drove of playful calves escaping from their pen and pouring onto fresh grass. Without warning a black figure was upon us cycling his stiff rusty bike. Us group of tots parted like the Red sea, leaving a gap in the centre of the road for the strange one to pass through. He reduced his speed by dragging one foot on the rough stony surface and, as he moved onwards, I noticed a little brown wicker basket attached to the bicycle front. Despite the warmth of the day he wore a long black heavy overcoat and wellingtons. While bicycle was then the common mode of transport, he seemed out of place, as everything about him was both black and ancient.

The following week we met him again, dressed in the same drab attire but this time, pushing his punctured transport. The wide black hat covering his head looked out of proportion and gave him a top-heavy and dwarfed appearance. He slowly sidled past the scholars, along the grass margin; head downcast and failing to make eye contact. He neither responded nor acknowledged our presence, even when being taunted by some of the more forward and bolder of the group. When it transpired that none of us could identify him, a fear of the unknown began to set in.

On reaching home I blurted out my strange experience to the silent attentive adults. That description fits only one person; "it has to be the Peddler", I was informed. I was warned that this inoffensive and simple man must be respected and should never be taunted by us children. It was explained that he lived in a two-roomed cottage near the railway level crossing on the road leading to the bog.

Each summer, this crafty codger would erect a skimpy scarecrow in front of his roadside dwelling. From experience, the Peddler knew that the passing carters, sitting on top of their load, couldn't resist using him as a target to aim their sods of precious dry turf at, until they knocked that scarecrow. Once the culprits were out of site the Peddler would collect the welcome fuel and re-erect his scarecrow to attract more free turf.

He peddled throughout the townlands selling his wares of thread, thimbles, needles, buttons and anything connected with sewing and patching. Most were glad to see him arrive and when he emptied the contents of his basket onto the table my eyes nearly popped out with wonder. Amongst the multitude of trinkim-trankims there was always a gem or surprise which the housewife 'must have' to complete repairs on some stubborn garment or other. He was never hard to pay, but sometimes clinching the deal went down to splitting the last halfpenny, at a time when it needed 960 farthings to complete a pound. Before leaving, the Peddler was always treated to whatever sustenance was going, usually a mouthful of tea and some bread and butter. From travelling house to house he had the news of the country, but never carried a word from one to another.

With the arrival of the 'Singer' sewing machine to many homes, purchased through the instalment system, he was finding it more difficult to compete. Eventually forced to diversify, he was reduced to doing odd jobs, mostly of a manual nature, for the farming community - cleaning out old sheds, spreading farmyard manure, mending fences and weeding the crops were his common tasks. I recall him digging the acre of potatoes in our 'last field', when he was long past his best years. Each day he dug about 12 drills, gathered and bagged the crop before manoeuvring each heavy sack onto his back and carrying them, one by one, the long distance to the farmyard, then up the steep concrete steps to the barn loft. While his reward was seldom in money form, he was always well fed and often departed with an extra shirt or surplus coat. This man of few words preferred to eat alone in a private corner of the kitchen and had no trouble in devouring a big mug of favoured fresh buttermilk with his plate of spuds and cabbage. And he was always handed a parcel of food to take with him before peddling homeward.

Not being house-proud, his humble abode was never treated to a lick of paint since the time he inherited it from his parents. The two front windows had long since lost their transparent value while the peeling door had to be dragged closed on its one remaining good hinge. The gaping hole left by the missing slates below the ridge, was a God send to the starlings that nested within the exposed cosy nook. Just like its occupant, the dwelling had seen its better days and it became a competition as to whether man or manor would outlive the other. As he aged, the Peddler took to foot while his derelict bicycle was dumped at front of his bungalow, now offering support to a crop of healthy nettles.

He was missing from the locality for some time before his absence was talked about. Eventually, news filtered out that as his house had become uninhabitable and because he had no living relatives, the Peddler was persuaded to enter the County Home for the elderly and destitute. He was left with no other choice but, probably to his surprise, ended his days in the greatest comfort he had ever known. His absence and demise closed a chapter, on a unique tradition in the local rural community, and left a void that remained long after.

Pigs In Flight

The expression "if pigs could fly" is posed in the belief that such occurrence is impossible and never known to have happened. Now I know different as I observed this phenomenon with my own eyes and had a grand stand, breathtaking view of one such occurrence. It took place some years ago when these animals had more freedom and were reared in smaller numbers, the pace of life was slower and rough manual work was tolerated as the norm on the farm.

I had prepared for the journey on the previous day, greased the cart axle and fitted the transport with its tall blue wooden crates, put the pony in the small paddock for easy catching and left the tackle in readiness. The following morning I got an early rouse, from the wind-up clock shrieking out its angry and unwelcome alarm call, and after a quick bite I walked out into the early chill of the dark winter's morning.

After harnessing the pony and attaching him to the cart I led him round to the pigsty and reversed the carriage against the sty doorway. With prearranged help from a neighbour we commenced the unpleasant task of manually loading the pigs one at a time. From experience I was aware that a pig is a very slippery animal, difficult to grasp and more difficult to hold on to while lifting its heavy bulk high enough to load onto the cart. We had the first pig raised and were about to place him in the cart when the pony, frightened by the pig's horrendous squealing, shifted the cart out of our reach, so the terrified pig had to be returned to his sty until the pony was calmed and tied on a shorter rein. Eventually after having to tolerate continuous screeching and repeated lifting we managed all eight pigs into the cart and secured them inside by fixing the tailboard in place. I seated myself above on the crate-to-crate wooden platform and with rein in hands, steered my cargo through our gateway and headed up the country road in the direction of town, five long miles away. I hadn't driven very far when faced with the steep incline of Tullyroe Hill and almost immediately it became obvious that the pony was having trouble in finding adequate grip to pull his heavy load up the steep incline. He had been recently shod and the new fittings were still shiny and lacked traction. In his backward sliding panic my pony suddenly reared up on his hind legs and propelled himself into a forward gallop. The sharp forward movement thrust the load of animals to the back of the cart and the resulting pressure ruptured the rope bellyband and caused the front shafts to rise skyward, almost lifting the pony off the ground.

The pony was now racing in a blind panic, the rear of the cart hopping off the road while the front shafts were almost perpendicular like a set of goalposts, except they lacked a net. As I watched, helplessly from my rickety and speeding crows nest and now clinging on for my life all eight pigs flew out, on their airborne journey into the darkness, through the opening that had formed when the back crate split under the pressure.

My pony continued on his mad wild gallop, while in the dark distance I noticed the silhouette of a figure on the roadway, and as I drew level a man emerged from the shadows and grabbed hold of the pony's head collar. While running alongside, the man eased the animal to a stop within a short distance.

It was my neighbour Paddy who had also been preparing for the pig fair when he heard the approaching ram-tar, and being an experienced horseman, was able to catch and calm my pony using his quiet and gentle words. I was never more grateful for his presence.

Having replaced the torn harness and secured the bellyband, Paddy eased the foam-coated pony around in the direction of my home. Through fear, I did not resume my place within the cart but walked alongside and lead the animal slowly back to the farmyard. On my return I was happy to see that all eight escapees were uninjured and had found their way back home to their comfortable sty. I presumed that, as considerable time had elapsed I could release my pony from his carriage, as it was now far too late for resuming my journey. However to my disappointment, I was informed that immediate income was required, as payment of the penal land rates were overdue, and so with a heavy heart and despite my shock and the lateness, I managed to reload my charges and set out once again, along the same road, and headed for the pig fair.

CR୫ଠ

Our White Cow Whinger

For as long as I could remember she had dwelt on our small farm, placid slow and bony but totally white in colour. In fact she was the only such colourful cow in our locality. No wonder then, that to distinguish her from our other five cows, we named her The White Cow as each animal had been allotted a title. In fact her full name was the White Cow Whinger because her usual greeting when approached by human company was that she emitted a low whiney welcome. She expected special treatment and she always achieved her wish because any attempt to speed or rush her would usually derive the opposite result - she would simply rust. At the time we didn't supply milk to the creamery, as there was no collection centre within reach of our farm. However all the milk produced was required for domestic purposes in feeding calves, providing for a large family which included butter making by dash churn. Anyone who entered the house during the churning process had to lend a hand in the operation by rotating the handle for a period, failure to do so would be considered as 'bad luck'.

In summertime we usually completed the milking out in the field rather than housing or driving the bovines to the restriction of the farmyard. This method was the then awkward, rustic way of doing things, but in those days, traditional ideas were slow to change on the farm unless conditions forced an alternative way. In turn each cow had to be coaxed into a corner and over level ground. Only then could the milker hunker down and place the white enamel bucket on the ground underneath the udder and, with his knee in touch with the cow's leg, begin the milking process. It was important to remain in knee contact in order to detect any sudden movement because if the cow began to move, or worse such as an attempt to lash-out at the milker and bucket, a rapid exit response was imperative to save the operator being sprawled on the ground with the precious milk washing over him. While there was no reward in crying over spilt milk, its lack meant a berating, black tea, no cream for butter making and deprived thirsty calves.

An occasional event that terrified the herd and upset the milk-pale was the arrival of the damaging warble fly. While its noisy presence wasn't obvious to the human ear, the herd always detected its distant approach and this had the effect of making the cattle stampede blindly through any barrier until they reached safety in some dark or sheltered oasis, often times near a well. When a bucket reached the full mark of the white frothy liquid it was covered with a clean cloth and placed on top of a nearby tall stonewall, to protect it from interference, while the second pale was being milked full. Then both vessels were carried home by hand. Always before leaving, the traditional completion would be fulfilled by dipping the index finger in the milky froth and make the sign of the cross on the cows back while uttering the farming prayer of "God Bless the Cow."

The White cow was the one who was always out of step by producing her calf each autumn and thereby kept the house supplied with milk during the bare winter period when her comrades were on production sabbatical. Our's was an arid farm devoid of piped water, well, stream or river. The wooden barrel-stored run-off roof water didn't last long in the dry thirsty summertime; therefore the cattle had to be walked some distance along the public road, to avail of the newly drilled public pump. The only exception to participating in that long walk was the White who insisted, by her slow actions, that she remain on the farm where the water had to be drawn to her by bucket.

It was early in the month, and before daybreak, on the day I ushered the Whinger onto the roadway and headed for the October fair in Roscommon Town. This was the first time, since she arrived to us as a calf that she stepped outside our farm gate and as I closed the barrier I mused that probably she would never re-enter her familiar surroundings again.

Carrying a reins and a bucket I directed her to begin the five-mile journey towards town and as I encouraged the cow onwards I thought of how her fourteen years made her old for a bovine, yet I was only a few years older than my charge. Despite our grá for this friendly and placid animal we couldn't chance to keep her any longer, because if she died from old age while on our property we couldn't afford the financial loss, and much as we debated it, there was no provision for sentiment within farming. At first our progress was non-existent to slow, as my cow couldn't resist feeding on the lush sweet grass growing on the long acre. Now and then she would dip her head into one of the many deep potholes in the rough stony surface and vacuum out a huge drink. When she had eaten and drank her fill I coaxed her into a faster stride and luckily at the crossroad I met up with a neighbouring farmer who was setting out with his four steers so we decided that two herds are better than one and joined forces. This made it easier to block off the many gaps; open gateways and side roads while the companion eased the cattle past the plethora of natural obstacles and barking dogs as we drove onwards.

By the time we reached the town it was almost bright but many other farmers had arrived before us and taken up the prime display areas to accommodate and show their livestock. Using one end of my reins I made a halter, placed it around her head, and tied the other end to the railings of that large empty building in the Town Square known as The Harrison Hall. I utilised the bucket to milk her and afterwards used the pale in keeping her well watered.

Similar to the other sellers I waited and waited hoping that some dealer would take an interest in my bony cow. While she did get the odd visual inspection and questions were asked about her age and milk production, I did not get any tempting offers.

In the afternoon an elderly gentleman approached me. He was so well dressed that his attire made him appear out of place as a jobber. Along with his black suit and tie he wore a pocket–watch and a neat hat and sported a handlebars moustache. Despite his urban appearance I answered all his questions except "I wasn't sure" of the bovines age. To satisfy the age requirement this small man attempted the normal practice of teeth inspection.

When he attempted to open the Whingers mouth, the cow objected to this stranger and the unfamiliar treatment, by jerking her head upwards and almost knocking him down in the process. Having learned an embarrassing lesson he left the age question unanswered. He then offered me sixteen pounds to purchase my cow, but as I was advised on leaving home not to take less than twenty pounds, I insisted on a price of twenty-four. I knew I was on shaky ground as his was the only bid I had received all morning, but nineteen pounds and ten shillings was his final offer before he began to walk away. When I decided to accept, he returned, and taking out a small tin box, he drew a red mark across her white head while insisting "Ill have to get some luck out of that" so I promised him that I would treat him right. He advised me to stay in charge of the animal until he returned later with the cash payment. In the meantime other potential dealers glanced at my cow but when the red mark was noticed they looked no further as that was the universal 'Sold sign' indication.

· While enduring the long wait, and hoping that the buyer would keep his word by returning, I was kept amused with the antics of the Cheap-Jack who had pitched his wares nearby. As always, in order to commandeer the best stand he was the earliest arrival at the fair. There he then spread his items of delph and aluminium goods on the hard surface. He used many rouses to attract the crowd and then humoured them into finding a need to purchase one or more of his household products, which he sold for a few pence less than charged in the shops. I recall watching a elderly man lift a chamber pot and ask in a timid voice "what price is this" when the Cheap-Jack pretended not to hear and ignored him, the potential customer repeated his question in a louder voice and only then, when the bystanders began to listen and take heed, did the Cheap-

Jack acknowledge him by replying "if you can fill it you can take it with you for nothing". The red-faced man made an empty-handed and rapid exit down the street to a howl of laughter from the growing gallery. Now the dealer knew that his business would reap the benefit through increased sales.

Eventually my buyer did return and I helped him chaperon the cow down Castle Street where he closed her into a small meadow beyond the houses. He then took a wad of pound notes from his breast pocket and counted out nineteen to me, while he retained the last ten shillings as his "luck penny". I was concerned as it was normal for the seller to decide, and the sum he retained was well above the usual figure. I had intended returning five shillings to him but now this wasn't to be. However I parted company with the dealer and had a last look at the White Whinger before walking back up the street with the precious nineteen pounds secured deep down in my pocket.

Normally as part of the fair, and when after the deals were completed it was the practice to go for a treat. The usual was a whiskey or a bottle of porter for the adults and a coffee and fluffy biscuits for the youngsters. I always looked forward to my glass of coffee, as we seldom kept something so luxurious at home, and to taste it made from milk rather than the usual water, was sumptuous.

As I walked passed the sweet shop operated by the elderly Kelly sisters I could see many of the dealers and sellers dining inside, while on some tables, glasses of hot steaming coffee and cocoa were visible. I was tempted to go in and order but the cost of parting with the hefty luck penny made such additional spending impossible. Walking homeward out the Athlone road I had reached Molloy's hill before any traffic passed but a small pick-up truck stopped and the driver, our local postman who was a part-time jobber, gave me a lift to the crossroad. I walked home the last half mile and it was only when I drew level with our farm that the sad realisation dawned; our placid White Cow Whinger was no longer part of the herd and had gone permanently from our lands and from of our lives. No amount of money would ever take the place of the White whinger.

CR℘

The Little Brown Hen

Over the years our flock of hens were allowed to reduce in numbers. Their supply of eggs and production of chickens was not as critical or commercially rewarding as was the case during our rearing in the black and white days. However, tradition demanded that we continue to maintain a flock to eat the waste scraps and maintain avian life in the farmyard. One from the flock stood out from amongst the others - the little brown one. She was the hen who seemed equally happy with human company as with her own kind. She always knew when it was our dinner time and would arrange her daily 'house visit' to coincide with our meal. On approach she would skulk outside for a while, then make a dart under the kitchen table, grab a morsel that had fallen to the floor, race outside and gulp down the food. In time she became bolder and spent longer and longer eating under the table. On the occasions when the half door was closed, to impede her entry, she would fly up onto its top ledge and make her appearance with a downward flap of wings to alight on the stone kitchen floor. At the stage when she had overstayed her welcome, some diner would open the door and shout "whist hen" while waving a threatening hand or newspaper in her direction. The usual result was that the little brown one would fly rapidly out the doorway, often dropping her beak-full of food from the fright.

On the day she failed to show at dinnertime, questions were asked about her absence. The conclusion reached was that she must have 'lain out' and was hatching her clutch as she had done in previous years, and later surprise us by leading a family of yellow little chicks which she proudly paraded homeward from her secret nesting place. On her third day of absence I began to worry about her safety and started my search around the farmyard including the garden hedges but, to my disappointment, found no trace of the bird or her nest. I crossed the stream to enter to the 'well field' and tramped through the long summer vegetation while poking the area with the pitch-fork handle. At first I noticed a few feathers scattered on the wet ground but as I followed the trail the clumps of loose feathers increased, and there lying near the corner was the remains of the little brown hen. This was a sad and serious situation that demanded a swift and permanent response to avenge this crime. There was no need for an in-depth inquest as it was evident who the culprit was - I had often noticed a fox cross at the bottom of the meadow. While he always strode with an air of innocence and indifference, I imagined that renegade must have secretly eyed the flock, over a long period, in anticipation of an easy meal.

Yet, despite the ever present and inherent threat, I had tolerated his presence without interference, but now that anti-social behaviour must be ended - the fox had picked the wrong hen and would suffer the consequences.

Time was on my side but I needed to get this problem solved at first attempt to pre-empt any efforts to repeat or escape. It was a cool evening with a slight whispering wind blowing past in my favour when, dressed in my camouflage dark green combat attire and carrying my double barrel and two cartridges, I edged quietly and slowly along the march fence until reaching the hollow where I merged with the foliage under the tall white thorn.

Having hunkered down I loaded the firearm and rested the barrels on the barbed wire fence at eye level, eased back the hammer and held my forefinger to the trigger and waited for the cunning culprit.

Darkness was challenging for prominence and a chill was setting in but the villain had made no appearance. It was almost time for me to admit defeat when a commotion commenced near the far headland and a pheasant burst forth skyward in panic from the waste ground. It flew away uttering a string of startled expletives in objection to its late disturbance, as presumably it had just settled down for the night. On peering into the fading light I noticed some tall weeds sway over and back and within minutes I came face to face with my quarry. Holding the weapon in a firm grip I lined him up through my sights and as he approached nearer I swear I observed guilt in his watery eyes.

I felt the cold mettle of the trigger on my forefinger and knew that if I squeezed it now and discharged the deadly cargo that rogue would never worry another hen. Suddenly he stopped and sniffed the air; had he become aware of my presence or was that his way of confronting the deed and apologising for his outrage? Next minute a comrade joined him both bobbing heads in unison. Almost touching they seemed to be in discussion and now I had a golden opportunity to deal with both thieves and solve the problem with one blast. From my secret perch I watched the unfolding scene. This scenario made me think again and so found myself easing the trigger into the safety position and lowering my firearm carefully to the ground. Springing to my feet I let lick with a mouthful of loud colourful language at them, causing both to bolt swiftly away, unaware that they had just evaded their well-earned sentence of capital punishment.

Hopefully my words of dire warning will remain, ringing in their ears, and convince them never to return or repeat their foul behaviour in my backyard.

I Met Her at the Maple Ball

It was October 1971 when I received the official order to get myself to Monaghan within days. I barely knew where that place was prior to the outbreak of the political troubles in the North. That issue gave Monaghan a rapid national and media prominence, due to its pivotal location within the Ulster turmoil. As I was attached to a small rural Gárda Station in Co. Waterford, the cross-country journey up to Monaghan was then a daunting undertaking. Having packed all my worldly goods, including my dismantled bicycle into my red mini minor I set out on a cold wintry day *en route* to my northern destination. Even though it was late when I arrived in Monaghan town on that stormy night, I was relieved to have reached that milestone. Now my final destination was only 4 miles away, but as I travelled, through the darkness, I thought the journey seemed much longer. This was because I was aware that I was near the border and so feared that I might inadvertently find myself driving into counties Tyrone or Armagh, in possession of Gárda regalia stowed in the boot. Eventually I reached the last house on the row in Glaslough village, which was to become my new accommodation. Despite the lateness of the night, the friendly landlady was still up and waiting to welcome her new guest.

The next morning I travelled the three mile journey to the village of Emyvale to commence duty in the Gárda Station there. From 1970 that station had experienced a major change from being a quiet one-person part-time rural Station to becoming that of a 24-hour opening. This alteration meant that the manpower increased to 30 and most were young, many in their twenties. The general agreement was that Monaghan was one of the best places to be stationed and I intended making the most of my time during my temporary spell there. It was an ideal location from which to explore the scenery both North and South.

At the time, Monaghan businesses were bustling due to the troubles, as people further north came to socialise and even book and celebrate their weddings in safety. The local dance halls and hotels featured the top show bands and the promoters were well rewarded with crowded venues, and the money poured in.

When one of my colleagues suggested that I should take a spin to sample the weekly dance in the village of Rockcorry one Thursday night, I readily agreed. I headed off in my ancient red mini, passed through Monaghan town and a further 10 miles south brought me to my destination. Even though there was a lack of dedicated parking at the dance-hall, it was easy to find a space as there were fewer cars then. I headed toward the sound of music, but when I put my hand in the pocket of my drainpipes, to fetch my red ten bob note, I found nothing except a big hole which my precious cash had escaped through. I retraced my steps back to my car and carried out a thorough search in my vain attempt to find enough change to make up the required ten shillings. However, when that failed, I spied my cheque book peering at me from under the car seat.

I made my way back to the Ballroom, explained my predicament to the doorman and asked if he would accept a cheque. His answer was a puzzled glance and he just ignored my request. When I didn't move away, two more officious-looking doormen appeared and gave me the poison eye. Perhaps they feared that I was intent on causing trouble. When I relayed my 'sad story' to them I was firmly told that it was against their policy to take a cheque as entry was by cash only. Despite thinking the battle was lost, I knocked about to allow them time to think, and after a private conversation between them, they relented. The deal was that if I produced my driver's license they would accept my cheque and allow me in. Luckily I did have that document with me and at last gained entry to the 'Maple Ballroom'.

It was an ordinary rectangular hall, mineral bar at one end and the band playing at the other. The ladies were bunched together on the right-hand side while the gents lined the length of the opposite wall. The ladies stood looking at each other, rather than across the floor towards their potential dancing partner, giving the impression that they were not interested in the proceedings. The men, on the other hand, couldn't wait for the whistle to blow, in the form of Big Tom announcing *"Your next dance please"*. While the ladies stood their ground, the men made a mad dash in wave formation towards their spotted prey. But the movement didn't always work to plan, as the strength of the swirling tsunami often took on a life of its own and pushed the willing suitor off course and out of reach of their intended target. Positioning yourself in the waiting front row was a slight help but it did not guarantee a successful landing. Sometimes, after good strategic planning when you did ride the waves to bring you face to face with your selected beauty, it was very humiliating to get a refusal. The crossing back, empty-handed, over that bouncy maple floor was a long and deflating journey. A customary retort to such a refusal was *"why didn't you take your knitting with you"*. However God loves a trier, and in my case I had my eye on my Cinderella for some time and wasn't going to let the night pass without making my case.

I noticed that she danced every dance, usually with someone different, but though late the night, all hope wasn't gone. The trick now was to watch and be in the appropriate position when the dance stopped so I wouldn't have to wade my way through at the next start. My plan worked to perfection and better still I was rewarded with a smiling *"yes"* from my chosen beauty. When *"your next dance please"* was called again I asked if she would waltz the floor with me again and she smiled another yes.

Luckily that was the last dance of the night, so despite all the waiting I had made my strike exactly at the right time. As it happened she lived at home on a road back towards Monaghan town. This presented an ideal opportunity to offer her a lift home, which happily she accepted.

I remember it being a very bright moonlit night and fortunately so, as in my excitement, when I started the car I couldn't find the switch to turn on the lights. They were different times then; lacking night traffic in that quiet countryside, so I drove homeward slowly by the light of the harvest moon. Luckily within the first mile I located the switch to activate my car lights.

With all the fuss I forgot to ask my new friend's name, address or where she worked so after parting I wondered if I would ever manage to make contact with her again. But fate and determination decided that we did meet and did marry a few years later.

CR&O

The Old Homestead

"Lonely I wander through scenes of my childhood
They bring back to memory those happy days of yore
Gone are the old folk the house stands deserted,
No light at the window, no welcome at the door"

This old John McCormack refrain relates a poignant story often very true to the reality of changing conditions.

After a long absence, I obeyed that inner voice and stopped outside with the intention of a temporary glance. Here and there, gaping holes had appeared as loose slates had slid free and lay in pieces on the ground. The old and frail house seemed to be eyeing its long lost occupant and inviting me inside with its strange appealing and vacant stare. I followed its lure and attempted to unlatch the narrow lawn gate but found it rusted firmly in closed position. Undeterred, I forced a path through the briers that had embraced the narrow style.

The deep matted vegetation underfoot had entwined, forming a cushion across the hidden concrete pathway, which led me to the front door. I twisted the knob and pushed, but the heavy wooden door refused to budge. I hopped over the sidewall into what, for many years, was our very productive vegetable garden where I toiled in tending to the crops.

Wandering round to the back, I was hoping to peek through the window into that quarter which once served as our good room. Not alone was the frame and glass absent but a huge jagged opening had been gorged out from roof to ground to create a way for the entry of an old grey Ferguson tractor now housed inside. It was parked centre stage taking the place where, for many years, our elegant drop leaf oak table held prominence. I found it hard to believe that this indignity had befallen our precious sitting room. In my younger days this room was out of bounds to us children, apart from certain short-lived exceptions, such as 'Station Morning' when the neighbours would gather in to hear Mass and take breakfast there afterwards, (we were in the era that required fasting from the previous midnight).This parlour was also kept conserved for special family visitors who arrived from England or the occasional yank who graced our dwelling, and would be quickly ushered within this sacristy to avoid the sight of other less decorated quarters. Except for Easter Sunday and a full week at Christmas time, we as children were not allowed to wander within its unique expanse. This was the only room in our dwelling which was capable of being locked, and when so secured the key was hidden beyond the reach of young hands in order to preserve and protect this hallowed area.

What a delight on Christmas morning to run 'in the bare ones' from the cold concrete floor of the kitchen onto the plush smooth warm carpet which covered and complimented the wooden parlour floor. A quick search and each child would find their present hidden behind a curtain, under a chair, or covered by a cushion.

These presents varied little from year to year, from playing cards, cap guns, toy cars; board games such as draughts, and snakes and ladders which were the norm. We were given strict orders with respect to protecting the good furniture and we knew that if we failed to obey, an immediate lockout would result and God help anyone who innocently broke a precious vase or caused damage. This embargo placed a huge restriction on our horseplay and so subdued our activity to playing board games, rather than our much preferred pastime of hide and seek behind the furniture. An abiding memory is that of a glowing heat from the blazing turf fire on the open hearth, while above, the mantelpiece was decorated with the berried holly which we children had pinched the previous week from a neighbouring farm. This raid was pivotal as the female berried holly failed to grow on our lands.

Now the multitude of twigs lying in the cold fireplace confirmed that the jackdaws had taken possession of, and made their home in this otherwise retired and smokeless chimney. The once elegant sideboard, which in its glory days, supported a large mirror and a display of fine vases, now lay dishevelled in the corner where even the woodworm had abandoned it. The old HMV wind up gramophone was pushed to one side, with its wooden cabinet broken to bits, while a few ancient vinyl records and a multitude of discarded gramophone needles lay scattered and rusting on the floor. Here and there a strip of wallpaper still remained in place despite the pervading dampness. Out of curiosity I prized open an old rusty biscuit tin and was surprised to find it full of ancient receipts, displaying the payments made in pounds, shillings and pence.

With my last searching glance, before I left this once happy and proud room, I did notice that two metal hooks were screwed in place high up on opposite walls. I recalled that these were the anchors for stretching the cord on which every year supported the arrival of new Christmas cards, placed hanging on display throughout the festive season.

I ventured into the old kitchen/living area and when my eyes became accustomed to the dark, I found the room filled with old farm implements.

Even the wide fireplace and both its hobs, where we as youngsters used as fireside seats, were in use as storage areas for buckets and tools. The old black crane with its adjustable hooks still remained waiting in place but it would never again be called on to support the huge pigs-pot of boiling potatoes swinging above a blazing turf fire.

I found it difficult to believe but had to accept that this house, which had been home to many generations, was now in fast decline and had entered the final throes of departure. I had absorbed enough and decided….. *"Twas time I was leaving, Was time I passed on"*.

Back to School

I was just stepping down from the ladder when the postman arrived and handed me two letters. They were both from the same rural school and the pupils Laura and Patrick had issued an invitation for me to come to their National School and relate my memories of border experiences during the recent troubles. My initial thoughts were that perhaps the younger generation were better served without the burden of such negative information. On second thoughts, if this topic was part of their school agenda, these scholars were fully entitled to be made aware on all historic aspects relating to and impinging on their native environs. As one who had lived through and experienced the side effects of 'The Troubles', particularly the inconvenience of road closures, checkpoint searches and diversions, I decided that perhaps I did have a duty to respond and fulfil this special request.

Another concern was that I wouldn't have enough information to fill the allotted hour. However when I accepted that pleasant invitation and stood before the eager students, I surprised myself with the river of dormant knowledge that was waiting patiently until coaxed out, spurred by the intelligent questions that tumbled from the young and excited pupils, anxious to learn more about their recent Irish history.

Growing up in the West of Ireland, the border, or Co Monaghan, just didn't feature for me. If either were mentioned it was as if talking about Timbuktu or Kathmandu. The late sixties and onwards changed all this innocence. While that area remained remote, the frequent news features and television coverage relating to the troubled Northern region often gave mention of Co. Monaghan and usually for all the wrong reasons.

My first work journey northwards was to Monaghan in 1971, when I arrived at my arranged digs in the small border village of Glaslough. The following day I was invited to travel to a dwelling into Co. Armagh, to make acquaintance with a family there. My work colleague, who was familiar with that area and its history drove through the village of Clontibret and parked within Co. Monaghan, just a few yards short of the orchard county. We completed our cross-border journey on foot over a surface of worn-down but clearly visible remnants of embedded metal spikes on the public roadway. This official imposition, a left-over from a previous troubled period, was my first introduction to the reality of what normal everyday living was like there and the related difficulties of life in a restricted environment, particularly with respect to the many cross-border unapproved roads.

As Derry City was then featuring frequently in news bulletins I considered driving there to have a look for myself. Its no-go status was drawing world attention, so to satisfy my curiosity I decided that it would be a shame to miss out on exploring this stronghold of intriguing events. Starting out from Monaghan town, in my red morris mini, the trip was uneventful until I reached the border checkpoint at Aughnacloy. There I was directed by a British soldier, with his rifle pointed at me, into a new custom-built closed shed.

Within that building, and under the shadow of many gun-barrels, I was made empty all moveable items from my car, including the spare wheel.

I was then made stand in the corner while my vehicle was hoisted upwards and thoroughly searched inside, and underneath, by army personnel. After what seemed like an eternity I was presented with an official document that I had to sign, agreeing that no damage was done nor property taken. Only then was I allowed to reload my items, drive from the shed and continue on my journey.

One and a half hours later, on reaching the Craigavon double-deck bridge on the outskirts of the Maiden City, I was once again stopped and ordered at gunpoint to drive onto the lower deck and enter another military cage. Having checked my identity documents the army put me through another vehicle inspection. When questioned about my final destination, my white lie reply was that I was travelling non-stop into Donegal, which seemed to appease my military questioners and they allowed me through without further ado.

Once out of army sight I wheeled to the right and within minutes, reached my intended destination of the no-go Bogside area. Its location became obvious from its tall land-mark Rossville Flats complex, towering over that part of the grey city and which was then often presented on the Television screens as the emblem of a war-torn Derry.

Innocently, I drove into this "no-go" area but I was immediately surrounded by children, who seemed to be aged ranging from 6 years up to 16, led by a few adults. I thought that many of these children should rather be at school. But as I quickly learned, these youths were policing their Bogside, as the official Police Force - the RUC - was not welcome and thus forbidden to patrol there by the local residents. The mob of youngsters demanded the production and inspection of my driving licence and insisted on poking their heads into my car, in much the same manner that I had experienced by the military searches. Only when satisfied, albeit bemused, that I was a mere tourist, would they allow me to proceed.

On parking at a location dictated to me by the youths, I took to foot to explore my new surroundings. While I presumed that all ground movements were being monitored from the military nest atop the Rossville flats, I could also sense being eyed from the native occupants within those crowded dwellings. I looked discretely around before sneaking a few photos for posterity. Later I decided to turn back through the checkpoint and face for home, but on my way out I was waylaid by the good humoured youngsters who forced me to stop by thrusting Hurley sticks against my car. This time they were insisting that I purchase some of their spent rubber bullets, at a price of a half crown. These bullets were stockpiled after having been discharged by the RUC at the locals, often causing severe and permanent injury to their target. We eventually agreed on a value, and closed the deal at two shillings a bullet.

Before I made the return drive back across the Craigavon Bridge I dumped the spent bullets, fearing that if the British Army found such items in my possession they might form a certain opinion leading to a prolonged military interrogation and perhaps free accommodation for the night. After a short military search I was directed to proceed and was delighted to drive away from the then dower and lifeless city.

It didn't occur to me at that time that a young man in charge of maintaining the 'peoples checkpoint' in Derry's no-go Bogside, would years later become the Deputy First Minister at Stormont.

In October 2012, forty years later, I found myself back in that city again and walking across that beautiful and recently constructed meandering 'Peace Bridge', connecting the nationalist city side to the loyalist Waterside across the River Foyle. This pedestrian link was constructed in more enlightened times for all the right reasons. The old intention of keeping Derry citizens apart was now altered to that of encouraging and making it easier for people of differing traditions to meet and discuss and do business with each other in harmony.

When I enjoyed my first dander across this silver structure I found myself immediately beside the former Ebrington British Army barracks, where an official plaque reminds the viewer that the 'Blackbird of Slane' completed some military service here before being dispatched overseas. That ardent Irish Nationalist and poet, Francis Ledwidge, was later to die soldering in a British uniform, on 31 July 1917 in Ypres.

While shopping on the Waterside east bank, the rain came on, causing me to take shelter in the salubrious Public Health Centre. I took a seat at the generous back window, which provided a panoramic view of the city, particularly the

West Bank. Immediately to my front, the majestic River Foyle flowed stately through the city, bridged to my right by the silver bird-like structure I had earlier traversed on foot. To my left, and beyond the railway station, stood the solid Craigavon bridge carrying its two tiers of traffic to and from the heart of the Maiden City. A lorry, now half way along that blue bridge, was labouring under the weight of a large horizontal Christmas tree; no doubt that tree would soon be secured upright and decorated with lights and Christmas bunting in front of the iconic Guild Hall.

No sign now of the drab and prison-like block of the Rossville Flats, that ugly tower of desolation and isolator of humanity, which had blighted lives and the city skyline for too many years. All had been demolished to make way for proper low-level and comfortable family dwellings. In the far distance the Creggan Cemetery stood out, bringing to mind all the tragedy and stories that lie within its green folds. The foreground offered a spectacular view of the majestic Derry Walls. During my 1971 visit these robust ramparts were out of bounds to the public. That elevated structure was then smouldered under reams of rusty barbed-wire and clusters of patrolling soldiers. Now the renewed bustling activity confirmed that peace and prosperity has returned to that beautified and gentle city.

CR80

Sean South and Mulligan's Safe house

One of my favoured outdoor pursuits is to hike through Ireland, exploring its scenic trails. For that reason I joined the Knockatallon Ramblers Cub which is based in North Co. Monaghan. Our walking club draws its membership from that host county as well as from neighbouring Co. Fermanagh. While the club can claim to enjoy the involvement of 50 enrolled members, we usually find that the actual walking group varies between five and a manageable twenty on any of our weekly walks.

Our quarterly calender offers a balanced mix of both local and more further-afield routes. Summer Sundays find us anywhere from Glenveagh in Co. Donegal to Sliabh Martin in Co. Down which overlooks Kilbroney and Rostrevor. Now and again we also plod over the panoramic Howth Head in Co. Dublin.

Our local walks take us to such locations as Mullyash in South Monaghan, nearby Sliabh Gullian in South Armagh, and Rossmore Forest Park, just outside Monaghan town. The heather-clad Sliabh Beagh, near the club's base in North Co. Monaghan, is a favourite with most walkers.

It was on one such local Sliabh Beagh dander that we arrived at Mulligans cottage and sat outside in the warm August Sunday sunshine to have our lunch. If this vacant, ancient and isolated cottage could relate its experience it would hold the listener spell-bound.

While it stands in Co. Monaghan, its back door opens into Co. Fermanagh. The cottage had been home to the Mulligan family for many generations. Why it was ever constructed in such a remote location and surrounded by marginal land is a mystery. In former times, when used as a family residence, Mickey Mulligan's cottage was known as a 'safe house' and was availed of as temporary shelter by 'on-the-runs' during political upheavals.

On 27 December 1956 a group of diverse IRA men rendezvoused in Monaghan Town and finalised their plan to carry-out what they termed "Operation Harvest" in the North on New Years Day 1957. They decided on travelling to Brookborough, Co. Fermanagh to launch a surprise armed attack in the police barracks in that town. Their usual target of choice was to hit a Crown property in the North, near the border, while ensuring that the chosen location had multiple available escape routes leading back into the safety of the South. However, in selecting Brookborough the party of 14 IRA men hadn't prepared for the possibility of failure nor of an easy escape route, if needed, for a subsequent hasty withdrawal.

In the early morning of that New Year's Day, the party armed with guns, ammunition and hand grenades set out from Monaghan Town. They commandeered a haulage lorry at a quarry near Aughnacloy and forced the owner to drive them, with their arsenal, to Brookborough. It was reaching dusk when the gang released their captive chauffeur and commenced their armed attack on the police barracks.

The hero of the disruptive battle, which lasted less than half an hour, was the barrack Sergeant named Cordner, who, with the help of his four Constables, pinned-down the 14 attackers and successfully defended his barracks. In the event, two members of the attacking party were badly hurt. Seán South, a native of Co. Limerick, received fatal injuries and another young follower from Monaghan Town, twenty-one year old Fergal O'Hanlon, who could have been saved had medical attention been available, was also destined to succumb to a premature death.

The remaining 12 attackers managed to clamour aboard the now limping lorry, and haul their two dying companions with them. However due to the battle-damage inflicted on the lorry, the lack of solid roadway and the RUC in hot pursuit, the IRA had to abandon the vehicle at Moane's Crossroads in Co. Fermanagh, and take to the unfamiliar and snow-covered terrain of Bragan Mountain. After a difficult slog through the darkness on that heather-clad bog, the party were unable to carry their dying comrades any further and were forced to abandon both casualties in a local turf shed within Co. Fermanagh.

The remaining 12 continued on foot across the Mountain, through no-mans-land, into the relative safety of Co. Monaghan. Once the escapees found their lofty bearings they headed for the Knockatallon cottage of Mickey Mulligan and after a long five mile trek, all 12 soaking survivors reached their destination. Once inside the homestead all were sure of a welcome, sustenance and basic medical attention in that 'safe house'.

The passing of the subsequent fifty years and harsh mountain weather took its toll on this long-abandoned and derelict dwelling, but it would have been fruitless and fool-hardy to attempt any improvements to it during the upheaval and the uncertainty of 'The 'Troubles'.

However, once the agreed 1998 Peace Process was established, steps were taken to renovate that former dwelling. While the restored homestead is not used as a residence, it is occasionally visited to serve as a reminder that we have come a long way from the turmoil and intrigue of the past, to the norm of peaceful days. The renovations to Mickey Mulligan's modest two-room cottage was completed and it was officially opened on Sunday, 3 May 2009.

Foiling the Border Smugglers

Take the road from Monaghan Town, through Heasty's cross and wheel to the right towards Ballinode. But just before that village, veer sharply over Connolly's Bridge and continue the extra two miles to Brennan's Cross, and it is now almost within view. I say almost, as due to its age, disuse and neglect, this roadside structure has merged with the greenery and has become part of the local rustic landscape. It's very existence could and does go unnoticed to the passing stranger, however on close inspection, the curious tripper would establish that this delicate building, fully intact with walls and roof, measuring 9ft by 10ft and 10ft in height could not be mistaken for a defunct calf shed.

Hard to believe that this, purpose-built, simple structure still survives despite the toll of the years, and mechanical changes from push bike to motorised transport.

On April Fools Day 1923 the Customs arrangement came into effect on both sides of the Ulster Blackwater River. The Irish version, governed the south side of the river, and the British imposition placed on the northern side.

This pleasant waterway, which previously served as a county boundary, now took on a new and imposing purpose, acting as a hostile and permanent dividing barrier. This new line through the Province of Ulster, separated Monaghan from it's sister counties of Fermanagh, Tyrone and Armagh and caused considerable loss, hardship and inconvenience to the inhabitants on both sides of the new and contested divide. This new situation gave rise to an attitude of "whatever you say, say nothing"; a strict rule which remains respected in border communities to this day. This sealed-lips practice ensured that no useful information of local smuggling was passed to the customs officers and also that no local could be accused by their neighbour of passing such information.

Initially, the custom posts along the new border were of a temporary nature. However when these structures were upgraded to permanency by concrete, the residents had to accept that their way of life and access would be curtailed and altered for the remainder of their lifetime.

The art of law evasion was acquired very quickly, and intricate means of smuggling were devised. Cover of darkness, covert river crossings and the few remaining unmanned derelict railway connections, were availed of as a means of ferrying goods to fill the vacuum of shortages created on both sides of the divisive gulf.

This tiny shy galvanized hut, at Brennan's cross, was to play a pivotal roll in overseeing the new local reality. Each morning, regardless of weather conditions, an appointed customs officer would cycle from his home, usually the four mile journey from Monaghan Town, place his private cycle in the relative safety of the bicycle hut, sign and date the official office register there before peddling off on his semi-circle rounds on the official black bicycle, complete with carrier and basket.

His daily tour took him around the maze of tiny unapproved roads, spiralling in and out of Co. Monaghan - the majority of which were closed to vehicular traffic by way of inverted embedded metal spikes - as well as the few that remained open.

The officers' duty was to spot check on local travelling public for possession of contraband and when any unfortunate victim was found at fault, the goods were promptly seized and later destroyed. Occasionally a Court prosecution and fine would follow. Any such removal would represent a significant loss and hardship at a period when locals existed at subsistence level.

In order to confirm to his superiors that he was out on duty, the officer would also have to cycle to a pre agreed point and meet up with a colleague, when each would date and sign the other's register.

Glaslough Village was often the rendezvous point for the Ballinode and the Clontibret officers. Occasionally, both cyclists would be surprised by the waiting presence of their supervisor who would countersign both registers.

On completion of his daily tour of duty the officer would return the official bicycle to its hut and secure the log book before locking up for another day.

On 1 January 1993, Co. Monaghan experienced a full 70-year circle by returning to its pre-customs period of 1923. Interesting to note that amongst the very few remaining tangible reminders of a bygone age is this small, ivy-clad, isolated bicycle hut at Brennan's cross, now reposing in quiet and abandoned retirement. However, with the complexity of Brexit raising its threatening head, is it possible that such upgraded constructions will inhabit our landscape once again.

Papal visit to Ireland 1979

Recent discussion concerning Pope Francis and his acceptance of the official invitation to visit Ireland in 2018 puts me in mind of another time and a former Prelate. Early on the appointed morning in 1979, when Pope John Paul II decided to honour our country, it prompted members of our family to head off for Drogheda, the nearest meeting point to our home, and jockey into best viewing position there. I didn't travel with them as I feared that the promise of packed roads and huge traffic jams would not suit my impatient nature. Anyway I could always watch events unfold from the comfort of our home.

However, an opportunity to be part of that historic occasion arose the following day simply by chance. The local taxi owner asked if I would kindly drive a load of pilgrims in his old blue Volkswagen van, to the Ballybrit venue. When I took the key and started out at daybreak the next morning, I wondered if his old motor was capable of carrying us to Galway City and back. On arriving at the agreed pick-up place at the Diamond in Monaghan Town to collect my delighted customers, it became clear that there was more than the maximum load of eight passengers waiting for me. Each traveller was armed with a fold-up stool and I presumed that, because of the unique event, the Pope would authorise special dispensation for overcrowding. Therefore I welcomed all 14 passengers as they climbed aboard.

As time was on our side we set off and continued at a leisurely speed. Our journey was lightened with plenty of passenger banter, rosaries and singing. Driving through the towns of Longford, Roscommon and into Co. Galway our journey went without a hitch. After Ballygar our pace was disrupted, and dictated to some extent by a slight build-up of traffic in front. Progressing towards the town of Mountbellew the leading convoy was almost at a standstill and when at length we reached Moylough, travel became a stop-go reality. As I was familiar with the Galway road I wondered if an accident was contributing to the slowdown.

When we eventually reached the junction, after the town of Moylough, where the road to Tuam is finger-posted straight ahead while Galway City is reached by veering to the left, I noted that all traffic were travelling the Tuam road only. Frustration was building rapidly until I spotted the cause of the traffic jam. A row of traffic cones were arranged across the junction, in a manner which seemed to have official authority. This blockage prevented the traffic from accessing the direct road towards Galway. I had one of my passengers lift some cones and when we drove through, he replaced the offenders and got back on board. I presumed roadworks were in progress further on, but hoped to charm my way through any later obstructions. Now I progressed unimpeded, with the road to myself on this national route. I motored with caution, as on rounding every bend I half expected to be turned back at a roadblock or confronted by a waving Garda ready to chide me for my foolish manoeuvre and my overcrowding.

Our next 20 miles were uneventful, and before I knew it we were out on the Galway N17 road and within spitting distance of our Ballybrit destination.

On reaching that point, unimpeded, I had to presume that some local yob, with a unique notion of humour, had placed the offending traffic obstruction and gleaned a warped satisfaction from misdirecting the Pope's faithful pilgrims. In any case, this unexpected hoax worked like a dream in my favour.

At Ballybrit we were ushered into one of the many temporary car parks and after choosing a parking place in the huge field, all my passengers alighted, and carrying their fold-up stools, scurried off to find a good vantage point. I didn't face the madding crowd but instead donned my coveted bright hi-visibility jacket and clamoured over the stonewall leading directly onto the Racecourse. I was aware from my previous similar exploits that the sight of a moving hi-vis jacket bestows a special camouflage and dispensation on the wearer, and also insulates them against awkward questions from marshals and security.

Easing steadily forward and with purpose along the race-track I expected that, on observing this stranger heading towards the Pope, the security would blow the whistle and either detain, chastise or divert me away. I continued to walk boldly up the course, very visible, but careful not to draw any undue attention and managed to reach the point whereby I could almost shake hands with the Pope. However I didn't push my luck quite that far, it was enough to enjoy a bird's eye view and share in the occasion on that beautiful and extraordinary day on 30 September 1979.

CR&O

The Auld Lammas Fair

At the Auld Lammas fair boys,
Were you ever there?
Were you ever at the fair in Ballycastle O
Did you treat your Mary Ann?
To some dulse and yellow man
At the Auld Lammas Fair in Ballycastle O

My answer to this well-known and melodious question is 'yes' - I was at the fair. My first sojourn taking my family to this pretty seaside town was in 1978, now 40 years ago.

I didn't carry a road map with me, so when nearing the town I was almost fooled on noting a large sign, which stated 'Last available car-park' before the fair. Luckily, I didn't trust the entrepreneurial chancer who placed that sign but instead I drove onwards. On my journey I passed many more inviting 'Last parks'. all competing for the passing business. Eventually my luck petered out as the public road was closed to all but commercial Lammas traffic. I was happy to pay the fee and accept parking in a roadside field as directed by the busy stewards.

Setting out earlier that morning from Monaghan I hadn't allowed for the heavy volume of traffic and the many stop and search incidents by the British Army, during the height of troubled times. This left me late and now with still a mile's walk to reach the town, I came within view of the colourful melee of horses, stalls and visitors. I was soon in the middle of and part of a throng of people going everywhere and nowhere, all at once. Despite the generous width of the streets, it was difficult to squeeze past the milling waves of humanity. With stallholders shouting the praises of their wares, loudspeakers blaring music and buskers holding court in alleyways, the resulting noisy blend was awe inspiring.

My first priority was to sample the famed Dulse and Yellowman, which as yet, I had savoured in song and story only. With this important purchase made, I found a free windowsill to sit on while nibbling my delicacies. The seaweed Dulse tasted acrid while the solid honeycomb Yellowman was hard to chew but sweet on the tongue. On this last Monday of August the sun shone hot from a cloudless blue sky, but this welcome happen-stance was easily rectified as everything imaginable including sun-hats were on sale right in the middle of Ballycastle's main thoroughfare. The pubs and eating houses were full to the lip with diverse Ulster accents, out celebrating their annual harvest festival.

Similar to the other visitors, I dandered up and down and zigzagged through all the streets to ensure that nothing interesting would evade my searching eyes. Here and there I made a purchase or two, mostly souvenirs to take home.

As the sun cooled and began to slant seaward I had to call it a day and retreat towards my parked transport. Many revellers had already departed while others had made arrangements to stay on for the morrow to complete their traditional annual two-day carnival.

At last I had sampled one of Ireland's oldest fairs that had originated as a livestock market and has endured without interruption, even during the 'troubles', for over 300 years. Had I been walking those same streets during the fair of 1898 I could well have rubbed shoulders with Guglielmo Marconi as he went about his work. He was there to view progress on the trials of establishing one of the worlds earliest commercial wireless signals.

Last year, after a gap of 38 years and due to retirement, I regained the freedom to return to Ballycastle. This time I set out a day early and was impressed with the shortened journey, due to road improvements and the lack of military presence or searches. In the morning I was delighted to find the Auld Fair has changed very little despite the passage of time.

The streets were as I had left them 32 years ago, bustling with young and old and the same colourful crowd and stalls with robust dealers, Evangelists eager to convert, and of course oceans of Dulse and Yellowman. I have made The Auld Lammas Fair part of my annual holidays but now I enjoy it for its two full days of madness and incidentally, I did meet my Mary-Ann but contrary to the song she treated me rather than I treating her. This lovely surprise happened on my journey homewards when I stopped, about four miles south of Ballycastle, and parked on the safety of private property to enjoy a snack. While feasting my eyes on the beauty of the Mountain terrain I was approached by a lady from the nearby dwelling. While half expecting a reprimand and a request to move on, I was instead treated to a local geography lesson and presented with a punnet of beautiful home-grown strawberries.

The memory of this kind and unexpected gesture, from a stranger, was the ideal experience on which to complete my short rendezvous in Ballycastle.

No Pub, No Pawnbroker, No Police:
Bessbrook' Quaker Code

Each time I passed along the A25 on my way to Newry, the brown finger post announcing 'Derrymore House' beckoned. Eventually curiosity got the better of me, persuading me to detour and wheel in through its long leafy avenue. At the end of the lane I found an elegant thatched cottage of status and charm.

On payment of my admission fee, I entered the historic property, now in the careful ownership of the National Trust. Having viewed the stately interior with its old-world mystique, I could well understand why something important would have come to pass here. In fact, prior to the political union between Ireland and Great Britain, in 1800, many pivotal details of the pending Act of Union were discussed, agreed, and recorded here.

Derrymore House, standing on the outskirts of Newry, in Co. Armagh, and surrounded by fifty acres of mature woodland, was built in the late eighteenth century. Originally the land was owned by the native O'Hanlon Chieftains, but this Gaelic occupancy changed utterly under the plantation of Ulster when their land was seized and became the property of the Crown. Subsequently it came into the hands of the ruling class and ultimately into ownership of the Corry family, who built Derrymore House on the confiscated lands. A member of that family, Sir Isaac Corry, served as a Member of Parliament for Newry, from 1776, and for the following 24 years. While resident there he was promoted to become Chancellor in the British Government. To accommodate his easy of travel and personal safety, a special road was constructed to enable him by-pass Newry Town, on his way to Dublin. It is still known and named as Chancellors road.

In 1859 the Richardson's, a Quaker family from Lisburn, who had taken over the linen mills in nearby Bessbrook, bought Derrymore House and its lands as their residence.

My new awareness demanded an immediate history hike to Bessbrook village.

On approaching, I was struck by this well planned, elegant and stately hamlet and its orderly wide streets and spacious square. I noted that the symmetric rows of solid tenement houses, constructed for the Mill workers, remain of such high standard, that all are inhabited to this day. Most of the buildings in the village are built of granite because of its abundance locally. There, I learned that Bessbrook is a mixed harmonious village consisting of Anglican,

Methodist, Presbyterian and Catholic denominations.

Famous in earlier troubled times as the most militarily fortified village in Western Europe, Bessbrook remains unique in being the only town of its size which does not host a public house. John Richardson, the new miller and enlightened Quaker, well ahead of his time, ensured the Quaker policy whereby the three P's – Pub, Police station, Pawn shop - remained absent from Bessbrook. His linen mills would not alone give full employment to the local population but his company would also provide them with their needs, in housing and places of worship.

In his opinion their environment would influence the lifestyles and welfare of the people, and Richardson's scheme included facilities for education, health and recreation. He encouraged respect and tolerance for cultural and religious difference and also believed alcohol was the main cause of poverty and crime, so its sale would be forbidden and consequently the absence of a Pub would negate the need for either a Pawn shop or Police presence. Therefore, with all their needs catered for, the residents would live a happy, prosperous and fulfilled life without need for recourse to any of the three P's.

Bessbrook owes its existence to the permanent supply of quality water, its proximity to Newry Port and the service of the adjacent Dublin Belfast railway connection. Its fame stretched abroad, through the loyalty of its workforce and quality of its linen products. The growing reputation of Richardson's practical idealism drew interested visitors here to view and to learn.

Richardson modelled his Hamlet on another Quaker settlement – Portlaw in Co Waterford - but Bessbrook, despite its growth, remains a model village to this day. The miller was handsomely rewarded for his generosity, as not alone did he spearhead a grateful workforce, but his prosperity allowed him gain ownership of Bessbrook village, the twelve surrounding townlands, and Derrymore Demesne.

In 1952, in a final act of benevolence, the Richardson Family handed over Derrymore House with its fifty acres, to the National Trust. Now it permanently resides, in their safe and caring hands, as an Open House and available for all to visit and enjoy.

Widows' Row

Similar to most other days, the pier at Newcastle, Co. Down was busy from early dawn on 13 January 1843. All the hard-working fishermen were making their usual last minute preparations before putting to sea. Weather conditions were good to fair and all the mariners were anxious for an early start to ensure an early return to port for a restful weekend. Some of the older and more experienced men, having scanned what they considered as a threatening sky, and combined with it being Friday 13th, decided to remain at port and spend the day repairing their nets.

The younger fishermen, who had dependents to support and were less superstitious of the 13th falling on a Friday, set out to sea in their normal jovial mood in their 12 boats, each with a full crew. Having travelled about five miles from port the party had hauled only a meagre catch and therefore a collective decision was agreed to push further out in the Irish Sea. Now almost six miles out, the fish-stock was found more plentiful and within a short time all boats had caught an adequate supply and turned for home. Shortly afterwards a slight snow-storm flared-up. As the flotilla continued its homeward journey, the soft breeze began to strengthen rapidly and a gathering fog reduced visibility to yards. Weather conditions worsened sharply and within a short time the cold wind reached hurricane level. The hapless craft were tossed about and flooded with water from the thundering waves and the crew had lost their sense of direction.

Meanwhile many concerned relatives had gathered on the quay at Newcastle, all worried as the boats were well overdue. Despite the storm, which was now lashing the coastline, two small rescue boats set out from Newcastle to find and assist the missing fishermen find there way back to port. Unfortunately no souls aboard the rescue party ever reached their stranded comrades but instead fell victim to the same cruel waters within a short time. In the end, only two boats, with their crew, made it back safely to Newcastle port. The remaining 12 craft and all on board were to perish in the freezing depths, during the horrendous weather conditions.

Seventy three brave fishermen were drowned on that tragic day. They left behind 27 widows and 118 children to grieve, along with many other dependents including elderly parents. The existing record's itemise the financial standing of the bereaved as *"of helpless and limited means"*, *"poor"*, *"very poor"*, *"wretchedly poor"*, *"daughter grown up but poor"*, *"dependent parents very poor"*.

In those days there were no widows pensions nor other social welfare

57

systems to assist those who found themselves without their normal income and therefore tossed into financial turmoil. An immediate high level meeting was convened in Newcastle, where representatives from all the leading sections of the community attended. It was agreed to establish a Trust whereby a collection would be taken up from the inhabitants around Newcastle and the resulting proceeds would be distributed to the bereaved, according to their immediate needs.

A surviving document indicates that substantial subscriptions rolled in immediately, not alone from all around Newcastle, but as far away as Belfast, Newry, Dublin, Derry and London. Topping the donation list was Countess Annesley, a landlord from nearby Castlewellan, providing the astonishing figure of £60, a huge sum in 1843. Most donations ranged from £10 to ten shillings.

The bulk of the fund was devoted to the construction of a row of 12 elevated dwellings on the Kings Road, all nestling under the protective shadow of Sliabh Donard. All 12 two-story houses are exactly similar and unique in appearance and each enjoys a clear view of the adjacent Irish Sea and Newcastle Bay.

When I visited these houses, a friendly resident was delighted to introduce me to her comfortable home in Widows Row. She informed me that all twelve distinguished dwellings, which stand as a lasting reminder of the Newcastle tragedy, are now listed under protective legislation which forbids any alteration to their outside appearance.

While many poems were written to commemorate that sad event, the one that encapsulates the tragedy best is penned by local man Mr John Cunningham of Maghereagh, Co. Down. Its titled "The Newcastle Fishermen":

The Newcastle Fishermen

It was a misfortune that happened of late,
The year eighteen hundred and forty-three was the date
On the thirteenth of January that fatal day
Those boats were well manned from Newcastle Bay.

Great praises are due to old William McVeigh,
That morning going out to the men he did say;
"This morning reminds me so much of fourteen"
Says he: "My brave boys in the bay, don't be seen"

They said to each other they could not be beat,
"There's no waves in the ocean can make us retreat,
Our lines they are strong and our boats they are stout,
For that very reason we will venture out."

Four miles they row Sou'-east from West Annalong,
To a landmark called 'The Bleachyards' where the waves they run strong
And for to fish haddock they joined in a fleet
And happy and merry together did meet.

The storm increased about twelve o'clock
When the ocean did foam and the billows did rock,
They hauled in their anchors to race for the land,
Each man standing ready with an oar in his hand.

Great praises are due to Captain Chesney's son.
In the midst of all dangers from the quay he had sprung.
He swam o'er the billows like Lysander of old.
And of young William Purdy he quickly took hold.

He saved him from drowning when death it was near,
And with a true valour made death disappear.
He dragged him along with the help of an oar,
And only for that he'd ne'er have seen Mourne shore.

There are some of them buried in the churchyard of Kilkeel,
And some of them buried in the Meeting-house field,
And some of them buried in Massforth as of yore,
Or lie quite contiguous around Mourne shore.

Thanks be to God who ruleth the sea,
And comforts the comfortless by night and day,
May He look after the orphans who often sigh sore
For the loss of their parents around Mourne shore.

The Yelverton Affair

It was a hardy March morning with a cutting wind whispering through the nearby trees when I arrived at the remote Killowen Chapel in the parish of Rostrevor. I had gotten word of a world-famous wedding that had happened there back 150 years ago, so I had to investigate. As I dandered around the locked chapel, looking for a plaque or marker, I was informed by a local that I would need to travel a mile further as the old chapel had long since closed for worship and had become what is now the local school. At the time, the quiet religious event on 15th of August 1857 had all the hallmarks of a hushed, almost secret wedding. However, within a short four years the union was to become the material of a sensational drama, exploding out in the Four Courts in Dublin.

In 1832 Theresa Longworth was born into a working class Catholic family in Edinburgh. Her mother died when Theresa was only a child so she was sent to a convent in France to be educated by the nuns. Her father passed away when she was 20, but left her a modest inheritance, which allowed her freedom to enjoy her many exotic exploits.

Charles Yelverton was an audacious, upper-class and ambitious Protestant from the Anglo-Irish tradition, with Co. Tipperary connections. It seems that when Theresa, still in her late teens, first set eyes on this dashing army Captain, and despite the age gap of 12 years, she was smitten and destined to follow him whenever and wherever he went. While Yelverton was pleased that this vivacious lady had a huge grá for him, he was more interested in his soldiering duties and did not respond easily to Theresa.

Eventually after much wooing, on her part, and when he did eventually ask her to marry him, she was delighted. However, because of her Catholic upbringing she insisted that they must be married in a Catholic Chapel and by a priest.

Charles held a different opinion; he would have preferred a simple quiet ceremony as he wished to have Theresa as a mistress rather than a wife, and therefore avoiding the obligation to support her financially. As a temporary measure and to ensure that she didn't loose her shining knight she agreed that together they would swear their loyalty to each other on the Bible.

Despite this secret ceremony, Theresa insisted that she needed them to go through a genuine Catholic marriage. While still protesting, Charles at last agreed to fulfil her insistence and both decided that Ireland would be the best place to find a willing priest. Arriving in Wexford in August 1857 they made many unsuccessful enquires. Dublin did not treat them any better and for some unknown reason they headed North and booked into a boarding house in The Square in Rostrevor.

Their next stop was the priest's house where they discussed their predicament with Fr. Bernard Mooney, the parish priest of Rostrevor and Killowen.

As both lovers insisted on a quiet wedding, this obliging priest agreed to perform the ceremony at the remote Killowen Chapel.

And so it was that on 15 August 1857 Captain Charles Yelverton and Theresa Longworth were pronounced man and wife in the sole presence of Fr. Mooney under the shadows of the protective Mourne Mountains.

On the surface, all went well but unknown to Theresa, the restless Captain had mixed ideas, and 1858 found him married again, this time to Emily Forbes - a lady of his own class and creed. This ceremony was sealed by a Protestant clergyman. In doing so, Yelverton overlooked the reality that he was already married to Theresa and his misbehaviour didn't go down too well with his jilted Catholic wife. Rather than sit back and accept the new situation, the sprightly Theresa set about defending her marriage. In 1861 she initiated High Court proceedings in the Four Courts, but not to be out-witted, the conniving Yelverton issued a counter-claim.

The resulting legal arguments which lasted for weeks, made daily headlines throughout the English speaking world. Fr Mooney, the Rostrevor celebrant was also hauled before the Court as a reluctant marriage witness and outlined his knowledge and involvement in the matter. In the end the Court held with Theresa Longworth and confirmed her as Charles Yelverton's lawful and only wife.

However Charles was determined to have his way and took his case to the House of Lords. As he presumed, his status and religious persuasion did impress The Lords, who make the decision in Yelverton's favour but on religious grounds, rather than on solid facts. The final outcome ruled that the marriage to Theresa was void, as their wedding was performed by a Catholic priest, which did not suit official mores of the time.

While Theresa Longworth lost the battle, she won the war in that subsequent to the outcome of the case, further discussion ensued. This eventually led to the enactment of the "Marriage Causes and Marriage Law Amendment Act of 1870". Under this Act, future mixed marriages celebrated by a Catholic Priest became valid and lawful, subject to the normal provisos of civil law.

'Uncle Jack' The Jovial Gent of Glaslough

On 18th April 2016, news tumbled out around Monaghan that the Patriarch of Glaslough had passed away in his 99th year, and appropriately in unison with the morning chorus. While I don't fit into the category of a regular funeral goer, this was a unique exception that I was not going to miss, representing as it was, the end of an era and a moment in history.

I met with Jack Lesley occasionally and enjoyed his genial company after his return to Glaslough from the Eternal City, over 20 years ago. My first encounter was on taking a phone call from a soft cultured voice asking if I could meet him at his historic abode - Castle Lesley - to discuss a colony of bats, which had chosen to nest in one of the stables. As a Wildlife Ranger with the Department of Environment, he also liked to sit and discuss our mutual knowledge of wildlife.

Having arrived at the quaint, North Monaghan hamlet of Glaslough, I drove through the gateway into the Castle grounds where, some year's later, Paul Mc Cartney and Heather Mills would be wed.

After a short journey along the gravel-crunching avenue, Castle Leslie came into view and on parking I noted a strikingly tall figure, standing as straight as a rush, at the ornate doorway. This immaculately dressed gentleman approached and in the same soft voice, and with a warm handshake, welcomed me into his Castle home. His friendly reception led to us sharing a pot of tea while we chatted about wildlife on his surrounding waterways and woodlands.

When he donned his elegant hat, sporting a long pheasant-feather, I accompanied him to the courtyard where we inspected the bat colony and identified the species as brown long-eared. It quickly became clear that Jack was an expert in bat behaviour, and had little to learn. Rather, he was my teacher. He then invited me on a walk through their maturing woodlands and took pride in naming the wide variety of tree species growing within the huge estate.

Afterwards whenever I happened to be in the Glaslough locality I made a point of driving into the hallowed Castle grounds in the hope of meeting Uncle Jack, as he was affectionately known, on his daily morning walk and use the opportunity to discuss some new aspect of local wildlife.

I was also interested in Jack from an historical angle, because I was vaguely aware of his military exploits abroad. However this was an area he was reserved in speaking on and his deafness in one ear also hampered easy conversation.

After spending his childhood in the idyllic Glaslough Castle and its environs, John Leslie departed to the UK to pursue his college education there. His brief stint included the study of history in Cambridge and upon completion of University he joined the Irish Guards in 1938.

After a period in London, protecting the iconic Buckingham Palace and the Tower of London, John became restless and decided to move on. 1940 found Captain Leslie in France leading a battalion of the British Army in opposing Hitler's reign of terror. Unfortunately Captain John was taken captive and confined as a prisoner-of-war for the remaining years of the battle. While he was not directly ill-treated by the enemy, the prolonged cold and hungry conditions imposed while in confinement, caused permanent damage to his health.

On news of his death I kept a close ear to the obituaries on the local Northern Sound Radio. The message indicated that Uncle Jack's funeral would be held at the nearby Glennan Chapel followed by a return to the Castle for burial in the family plot, while the Castle itself would remain closed until 12 the following day.

On Wednesday 20th April I arrived at the Chapel well in advance, wishing to take in the approach of his cortège and glimpse any surprises that Uncle Jack may have written into his final arrangements. When the funeral procession made its appearance, along the rustic road, it was clear that his final journey was one of style. The Chief mourners led the way in a carriage pulled by a pair of black horses while the coffin was transported, to St Mary's Church, in a glass-enclosed Victorian hearse by a brace of matching black horses taking the strain.

Jack timed his last surprise for the end of the Ceremony, when the speaker announced that all present were invited and encouraged to follow the procession back into the Castle grounds, attend Jacks burial and dine there afterwards. This additional treat came as a complete surprise and of course I was happy and grateful to avail of the invitation.

We followed the hearse along the winding lake-lined private avenue to a prepared grave beside the ancient churchyard wall and there, to the haunting sound of an Uilleann pipe, Uncle Jack was gently lowered to his final resting place. After a rendition of *"Will you go lassie go"*, from the fulsome tenor voice of Uncle Jacks grand nephew, we filed towards the Castle entrance.

Once there, all were treated to sandwiches and generous chunks of cake. Tea, orangeade and Champagne flowed freely. All was dished out by the friendly staff, exactly as dictated by Jack in his final wishes.

Despite enjoying the prepared banquet, it was sad to accept that Sir John Leslie, the 4th Baronet of Glaslough and Pettigo, had departed and was unavailable to mingle with his guests as he would have wished. Uncle Jack would have taken great delight in witnessing the outcome of the surprise he created, on that unique warm spring afternoon.

Letterfrack's Dark 'De'formatory

It was in the Autumn of 1970, and during my first year of service, when I was detailed with another Gárda colleague to accompany a passenger on his way to Letterfrack. Our charge was a silent youth of about 15 years. This unfortunate child had been sentenced to Letterfrack as he had been a repeat offender of petty crime around Waterford City. While he was known to the Gardai as a wild one, he did not pose a dangerous threat to any person. At the time I barely knew where Letterfrack was, except that it existed somewhere in Co. Galway. All four, the taxi-driver, my colleague, the offender and I, set out early on a wet February morning to allow us reach our remote destination and return to Waterford City the same day. The further we travelled on that long journey, the more uncomfortable I felt as I instinctively knew that the Court's sentence was much too harsh, particularly on one of such tender years. The word 'Letterfrack' was enough to instil fear into any listener as it inferred an isolated place of punishment where those in charge were more in need of reform than the inmates they supposedly supervised. To impose a penalty which separated a vulnerable youth so far from his home, his parents and acquaintances was cruel, unreasonable and excessive. As it transpired, this long and tiring journey was then one of the longest distances I had travelled within Ireland. At each stop along our journey the youth was placed in handcuffs. This restricting action, while unsavoury, was a mandatory requirement.

On reaching the village of Letterfrack, we were chaperoned, now in the darkness, through the "Reformatory's" large iron gates by two Christian Brothers. We were then invited into the industrial school building for a meal; except for the youth, who was marshalled away and out of our sight for ever, to serve his time. Within an hour we were back on the road again, heading for Waterford, now reduced to three in number.

It was in the summer of 2017 before I found myself back in that area again. Now retired, I travelled with my wife and daughter to visit Connemara National Park. We enjoyed walking the park and scaling its highest peak - Diamond Mountain - on that beautiful warm day. While viewing the exhibits within its interpretative Centre I was fortunate to meet with Helen, a friendly member of staff, who was a mine of local information. When I asked about the former Letterfrack Reformatory, she recalled that in her national school days the secluded industrial school was active but separated from the local community. She explained that since the departure of the Christian Brothers and the closure of the Reformatory, the building has become a third-level centre of learning. She also mentioned that one aspect that remains as a constant reminder of those grim and harsh days, is the adjacent graveyard. I walked across the wooden footbridge which took me down the short narrow lane and in through the small gateway, to pay my respects.

Within that silent tree-sheltered sanctuary I observed rows of stone plaques, each etched with the name of a student who died within the walls of that austere institution. The ages ranged from 5 to 16 years and it made me wonder just why they died and the cause of each death. During its active service from 1887 to 1974 a total of 2819 children entered through its captive doors and at least 147 of these children were destined to die and be interred in its cemetery grounds there. Many died through neglect and others because of the harsh physical, emotional and sexual abuse imposed on them by the very adults who were duty-bound to nurture and protect those helpless children.

The sad fact is that this remote an unsuitable institution was always surplus to requirement. In 1884 Dr John Mc Evilly, Archbishop of Tuam purchased the buildings, which at that time were officially certified to accommodate not more that 75 people. The Catholic Archbishop embarked on a recruiting campaign to fill these places with boys "in need of reform" but initially his unfounded suggestion was ignored by the State authorities. However, when the priest persisted, the State relented and assisted in opening the complex as a Reformatory with a promised intake of 75 boys. The overall depraved operation was entrusted to the governance of the Catholic Church, in the form of the Christian Brothers as guardians, tutors and enforcers.

When it opened in 1887 the boarders consisted of boys up to 16 years of age who were sent there by the Courts for committing petty crime. More came as homeless youth or orphans while others were placed there by a family member who couldn't manage or didn't want to be bothered in rearing their forsaken offspring. Once inside the clutches of Letterfrack Reformatory, there were neither holidays nor release until the student reached the age of 'adulthood' at 16 years, and while within, those inmates were denied recourse to any justice or access to the justice system. Worst of all, the emphasis was on a diet of inadequate food and a daily dose of hard labour and punishment, rather than education. Most inmates were destined to serve their time without ever receiving a visitor during their years of incarceration.

What became of the wayward Waterford child that I escorted to that hellhole I will never know. That unfortunate youth didn't even seem to have a name.

The Cahan's Presbyterian Exodus

The tide was ebbing as we walked along the bank of the Clanrye River, but despite its lowered level, this babbling water which forms the county boundary between Co. Armagh and Co. Down, lightened our journey. We continued walking atop the high protective sea embankment and arrived at the little rustic stile which led us onto the Newry to Warrenpoint road.

There, by prior arrangement, and to satisfy the obligations of the Parades Act, we were greeted by three friendly members of the PSNI. They halted the speeding motor traffic and ushered us, like a flock of ducklings, across that busy dual carriageway to the safety of the opposite footpath. Contrary to the forecast from the met office the weather had turned, and with a cold wind had begun to bite. The mist had matured into an ugly wet companion of a steady downpour as all 15 pioneers plodded on towards our final target.

A further three miles and our spirits lifted when the silhouette of the ancient stone-built Norman Castle at Narrow Water came into view. This iconic monument was a welcome marker, and on spotting it we quickened our step and all of us wheeled into the avenue on our left and up the stone steps to enter Narrow Water Castle. Once inside, we were welcomed by the owner, Mr Hall, and invited to dump our wet gear before being ushered into the great dining room. There a blazing fire and lovely meal greeted us while mellow music, provided by a local group of fiddlers, sweetened the digestion.

We had now completed the fourth and final tranche of our fifty mile walking journey, starting in mid Co. Monaghan and ending at Narrow Water, Co. Down to commemorate those Presbyterians involved in the Cahan's Exodus two hundred and fifty years earlier in 1764. Our cross-community group was following in their foot-steps in recognition of the hardship they endured in their difficult and last poignant journey on Irish soil.

From the late sixteen to early seventeen hundreds large groups of Presbyterians poured into Ireland. Forced from their native Scotland through persistent religious discrimination, they assumed this country would provide them a better option to practice freely.

Many arrived in the Ballybay area of Co. Monaghan, to join their co religionists who had settled there previously. They engaged in farming and laboured in the flax growing business which was flourishing all over Ulster at that period.

Their fold must have adapted to Irish custom very rapidly, as dissent spread within their tight-knit community, particularly with respect to their varying views of religious observance.

The resulting schism caused a sizeable group of about 300 souls to depart the Ballybay congregation and set up their new branch at a remote rural setting between Ballybay and Corcaghan, known as Cahan's. Here in 1740 they erected their meeting house and within a short period, having found their feet, the congregation appointed their own Minister. They choose well in Dr. Thomas Clark, a born leader and no-nonsense fellow Scotsman. Similar to all his co-religious he detested having to pay tithes to the Official Church of Ireland. Because he also had stubborn nationalistic tendencies, he refused to submit to the Act of Allegiance, and suffered spells of imprisonment for his principled stand. Undeterred by this separation he continued to represent and advise his followers even from within the bleak walls.

Despite having left Scotland because of the effects of the depressing penal laws, they now found that the exact same conditions militated against them in Ireland.

After the death of his wife, Minister Clark became restless and decided that there was nothing only a bleak future for his flock if they remained within Co. Monaghan, or Ireland. In May of 1764 Thomas Clark and about 300 of his followers made the momentous decision to depart and sail for New York.

While their exact land journey is not known, it is certain that the route from Cahan's to Narrow Water would be by way of difficult minor by-roads only. Their journey took four days to complete. Some would have travelled by horse-drawn carts, while the most able would have walked alongside.

What happened to their excess property on reaching the port is unclear but most likely all except basic hand luggage was sold at a reduced rate before they embarked, to supplement the cost of their sea passage. On that momentous May day all 300 men, women and children, boarded the 'John' at Narrow Water, Co Down, waved good bye to Ireland and sailed away in that basic ship, on an uncomfortable passage, to a new and unsure future.

Eight weeks later, in mid July 1764 all 300 members found themselves in New York. They remained there only long enough to 'catch their breath' in their adopted country, and then moved on to New Perth. For most, this became their new home where they bought land and settled among other Presbyterians who had sailed to America from the Scottish Highlands a generation previously. However a small, more adventurous segment parted and travelled on to South Carolina, where they put down their roots.

Pastor Clarke decided to remain with the main bunch in New Perth. However in 1782, when his feet itched once more, he bade farewell to his flock at New Perth and travelled to join the South Carolina sect. There, ten years later in 1792, their beloved leader Dr Thomas Clark died.

Not satisfied with our one-way journey, it was decided that our mixed group would take on a return walking journey from Narrow Water to Cahan's. Again we divided the task into four separate journeys.

In discussing our diverse culture, I asked one Presbyterian fellow walker to identify any major difference between his religion and my Catholic upbringing. His jovial reply was that "we Presbyterians keep the Sabbath, we keep the Commandments and we keep anything else we can get our hands on". I assured him that this attitude confirms there is little difference in our respective behaviour.

Our small troop did complete our sojourn in harmony and cemented a lasting friendship across the religious divide.

Cultra's Hand and Pen Orange Hall

Now that I am done with paid employment and reclaimed my precious time, I relish the freedom of choosing my priorities. One of my interests is to engage with those who hold different views and those who practice different backgrounds. Joining the local network was the ideal means to achieve this cross community and cross border meeting of minds, particularly with our new friends from Co. Armagh.

One such joint get together took place in the Transport and Folk Museum in Cultra, near Hollywood, Co. Down. On arrival we were met by Tom our guide. Following his hearty welcome and introduction to the history of the place, our host informed us, in his deep and witty Ulster accent, that the Museum was the brainchild of a Mr Evans who, back in the early fifties, had the foresight to realise that old ways, particularly farming methods and lifestyles, having stood still for decades, were beginning to change very rapidly. Horse power and hand tools were being abandoned to make way for motor-driven machinery. Also, the new power of electricity, together with modern materials meant that older buildings were being replaced with new designs. Therefore, it was time to consider the setting up of an Ulster Museum to maintain and display a sample of items used in a bygone era. This resource would enable future generations experience a glimpse of the past in one setting. Mr Evans and his scouts spent much time travelling throughout Ulster making enquiries and spotting potential exhibits for their imaginary museum. They also went about lobbying the politicians to ensure that his daydream could became a reality.

Eventually, that gentleman's persistence met with success when an Act of Parliament was passed in 1958 providing for the creation of the Ulster Museum's Centre. That huge step gave permission for the purchase of 200 acres, of the former Kennedy estate, as the ideal location to house Ireland's first official Transport Museum to be known as The Ulster Transport and Folk Park. It opened its doors to the public in 1964.

All nine Ulster counties, with the exception of Co. Cavan are represented here, through donations of buildings and abandoned accoutrements, which now stand on show in this leisurely oasis.

On that blustery day it was a treat to dodge into the various buildings and see what each had to offer. The old Courthouse, transported from Cushendall, was bare and as cold as during its working days. Likewise the old National School, relocated from Banbridge, Co. Down, brought back memories of drab, bleaker and more innocent school days. In the warm forge we were given a lesson on how to fashion a horse-shoe from a straight strap of metal, hot- reddened from a raging coal fire.

A short walk and the lovely aroma of burning turf drew me into one of the larger houses. There a blazing cheerful fire danced under a solid swivel crane while a boiling kettle hung over the jumping flames.

This was the Manse, an exile from Toomebridge, and as luck would have it the lady of the manner, dressed in period attire, was baking buns on the old hearth griddle. As I watched the raw batter change from dough-white to a lovely attractive mouth-watering brown, I dallied there in the hope that the cook might need a taster to sample the completed dish. Sure enough she invited me to help myself. I obeyed and lashed on the waiting butter, which added to the contentment.

While each of the 50 or so buildings there have their own unique story on offer, I headed off to view the old farmyard, but as I rounded a bend I was stopped in my tracks by the sight of a tall rectangular structure. I had seen this building previously, standing in a different landscape - but where? Measuring approximately eighty feet by fifty, this plain but solid house was simple in design.

I soon realised that it was the same Orange Hall, transplanted in 1990, slate by slate and stone by stone, from its foundation of over 100 years in Corbeg, Silverstream, Co. Monaghan. With each item of the structure carefully numbered, it was conveyed the seventy miles and reinstated in its new home exactly as first built.

Originally erected around 1840 and renovated some sixty years later, it was known as Hand and Pen Orange Lodge No. 597 and stood halfway between Monaghan Town and Middletown in Co. Armagh. This pivotal location was carefully chosen as, in its heyday; about 80 members of the Orange Order resided in that catchment area. However, history relates that with the onset of the Great War, many of the men-folk departed to fight for King and Country, some of whom were destined never to return home. Their numbers were further depleted when partition's dividing line created a permanent and damaging gulf between Co Monaghan and Co. Armagh.

After hosting its final Orange Order Parade on 12 July 1931, the Hand and Pen Hall was no longer used, or found suitable for meetings or social Orange gatherings. Its costly upkeep also proved difficult for the shrinking community of brethren who continued to reside nearby. The building, which remains void of electricity, struggled on until the late 1980s when, by generous decision, it was signed over to the ownership of Cultra Transport and Folk Museum in Hollywood. Detailed plans for its transfer were commenced and by 1995 the exiled Hall took its completed and privileged place among the other Ulster show-pieces.

Dan White's Dander

We had reached the half way mark of 'Dan White's Dander' when our guide announced that it was resting time. With each of my fellow walkers, I sat myself on a dry protruding rock as the surrounding ground was still covered in morning dew.

Undoing my backpack, I joined in the communal snack. The man sharing my rock seat had come from Germany. The girl on my right from Co Fermanagh was the first to break into song and this encouraged other amateur artists to follow suit.

In the distant north east, the bulk of Sliabh Donard, which I had scaled last year, stood proudly against the blue sky. Further to the east, the Isle of Man came into view and to the south east, Lambay Island was visible. We had reached the pinnacle of our dander on that clear and perfect day. Earlier that Sunday morning my family and I had arrived in the magical village of Rostrevor. There, as part of the annual Fiddler's Green Festival in July, we joined the hardy band of seasoned festival-goers, some new faces and others I had met on previous mountain outings. Before setting off, our guide was resolute in checking that all involved wore adequate and suitable gear. The all-clear was given and we were led along the roadway for some distance and over a stile to commence our mountain challenge.

Our group were walking to commemorate the memory of a gentle soul who haunts the local terrain. The late Dan White lived alone in his two-roomed home on the slopes of Sliabh Martin. The skeleton of his derelict home was still visible as we walked past.

Dan, a sheep farmer, grazed his flock on commonage over the Mournes. Being self sufficient, he seldom ventured far, but once a week, rather than go by way of the busy Kilbroney Road, this retiring gentleman preferred to reach Rostrevor by 'dandering' over the peaceful mountain, and accompanied by his faithful dog, Shep, Dan would emerge onto the road at the foot of the village. During his short visit, he would purchase his rations and after a 'quick one' in the local pub, he would retrace his steps over the difficult five-mile mountain terrain, bound for home.

Following our short elevated rest, the order was given to arise and proceed so as to arrive on time for the Cloughmore games. This ancient re-enactment, which included the throwing of the 'caber' by kilt-cladded hefty Scotsmen, competing against the natives, took place beside the elevated and historical regional landmark known as the 'Cloch Mór' ('big stone' in Irish Gaelic), balanced atop Sliabh Martin which comprises the southern end of the Mourne Mountains.

Legend dictates that this round shaped stone landmark, visible for miles around and estimated to weigh 400 tons, was thrown from Co.Louth across Carlingford Bay by that famous Irish mythical giant - Fionn MacCool - and landed at its pivotal and precarious resting point in Co.Down.

When the games were over, all were led to a clearing in the adjacent forest to a place known as Fiddlers Green. Here, musicians entertained us with instrument and song, and the weary walkers took a welcome rest on the freshly cut meadow and feasted on the remaining refreshments.

Another hour passed, and our guide invited us to follow him so as not to miss the open-air concert in Rostrevor Square.

Our descent of the mountain provided not alone a splendid view of Rostrevor and Warrenpoint, but also of south Armagh and Omeath and at one viewing point, our guide pointed across Carlingford Bay to the profile of a large human lying in rock formation atop Sliabh Foy on the Cooley Peninsula in Co. Louth. The hibernating giant Fionn MacCool no less.

All-in-all an unforgettable sojourn was had and the next Fiddler's Green Festival is already marked in the diary for next July, when acquaintances will be renewed.

CR SO

Victoria Crosses

Since its inception in 1856, the Victoria Cross has been awarded to thirteen hundred and fifty individuals. The Cross itself, named after the British Monarch, is made from bronze, recycled from a Russian Canon which was captured during the Crimean War.

Fashioned as a Maltese Cross bearing the words "For Valor" the recipient's name is recorded on the reverse side. It is a plain, simple medal, lacking in any commercial value but one of the most coveted of all military awards and the highest and most prestigious available to British Commonwealth Forces for gallantry. It is bestowed by virtue of merit, without distinction to rank. In theory, gender or nationality is not an obstacle, but in practice and in the early days, being female, Irish, or serving as a Catholic Chaplain prevented it's winning.

Nevertheless approximately one hundred and fifty Irish-born soldiers and another fifty or so born abroad of Irish parentage did achieve success. This amounts to a remarkably high percentage of the total number of Irish who served in the British Army. However the Cross has never been awarded to a woman.

The first recipient of a VC Cross, Charles Lucas, was Irish through his Castleshane, Co Monaghan connection.

The second recipient was also Irish, Luke O'Connor of Co. Roscommon. Indeed, every Irish county, with the exception of Longford, can claim receivership of this unique award. Dublin holds the record at 18, followed closely by Cork at 17. Monaghan, with 6 VC's, is above the average rate for its sister counties in Ulster.

The latest to win a Victoria Cross was Irishman James Magennis, born in West Belfast in 1919 who commanded a Royal Navy submarine during 1942-45. He returned to civilian life in 1949 and is interred in Halifix, where he died of natural causes, in 1986.

Some time ago when caught in a traffic hold-up in Lifford, Co. Donegal, I decided to abandon the car and take to my hobby-horse, that of graveyard inspections. A short shanks-mare took me to Clonleigh Church of Ireland and cemetery where I came across a tall substantial headstone, erected to the memory of *George* Gardiner *VC*. The inscription also confirmed that he was born at Warrenpoint, Co Down in 1821. Having fought in the Crimean war, where as a 34 year old Sergeant he gained his VC Bravery Award, Having retired from military service, he died in 1891 at 70 years of age.

Prior to this discovery I had been aware of a David Nelson, born at Derraghland, Stranooden, Co. Monaghan who had fought in a British uniform against the German occupiers in France. While there, he was wounded and taken prisoner, but within days managed to escape.

He died shortly afterwards from his war wounds and was buried in Lilliers, France in April 1918. He too was granted the VC for his heroic endeavours.

This knowledge awakened an interest in this military aspect, in particular with respect to the holders of Victoria Crosses with a link to Co. Monaghan. I found that as well as David Nelson there are five other Monaghan men who have been awarded the Victoria Cross.

Charles Lucas 1834 to 1914, was a member of the landed gentry who had a Castleshane connection and was the first ever winner.

Francis Fitzpatrick of Tullycorbit 1859 - 1933, fought with the Connaught Rangers in South Africa.

William Temple, 1833 to 1919 - this surgeon, a native of Monaghan Town, soldered in New Zealand .

William Traynor 1870 – 1956, while born in England was of South Monaghan parents and fought in the Boer War.

Only 19 of these Irish born recipients of the VC are buried in their native Country. One of those, *Thomas Hughes,* hails from Broomfield, Castleblayney. Co. Monaghan.

A most unlikely and deserving winner was Thomas, born on the 10th of November 1885 at Coravoo, Castleblayney, Co Monaghan. He was the eldest of five children, to Rose and John Hughes, owners of a small less prosperous farm. Thomas had three brothers: John, Daniel, Patrick, and one sister Annie. On leaving national school early, he worked on the family farm, as was then the custom for the eldest son.

In 1915 he travelled to Dublin to support his county football team at Croke

Park. This was his first visit to the city and while there, Thomas was inveigled, while passing a recruitment stand, to join the British Army. So it is said that he went to Dublin as a football spectator, but joined the Army and failed to return home. While the Hughes family was of a republican persuasion, Thomas viewed enlistment as an outlet to escape dire poverty that then pervaded the country, and as a means to explore and pursue adventure.

He joined the army as a Private in the 6th Battalion of the Connaught Rangers and after six weeks basic training in Dublin, was posted overseas with his regiment, to fight in the battlefields of France and Belgium. During this period he was promoted to the rank of Corporal.

On 3rd September 1916 at the Somme, the Connaught Rangers were ordered, as cannon fodder, to take the lead and advance on the enemy, but were penned down under a hail of fire from a German gun-position. Corporal Hughes, lacking orders, broke from the line and advanced alone under heavy fire towards the enemy line. Whether through bravery or an act of folly, he single-handedly attacked the position, capturing the two machine guns along with its seven German operators.

Despite his success, Thomas suffered a leg wound which necessitated part of that limb being amputated. When he returned home after his adventures, the political climate had altered dramatically and sadly his status and that of his medal was not recognised during the remainder of his frugal lifetime. As his limb injury rendered him unemployable he whiled out the life as a character around Castleblayney and became affectionately known as the VC *Hughes*. He remained a bachelor and died on the 4th Jan 1942 and lies buried in his native Broomfield near Castleblayney, beside his younger brother John. The inscription on Thomas Hughes headstone bears testimony to his achievement.

Uniquely he is the only one of the six Monaghan VC recipients interred in his native county. It is ironic that while Thomas was winning his award fighting for the British in a foreign land, his brother, John, a member of the IRA was confronting the British in Ireland. Unfortunately in the late sixties Thomas's VC medal was sold and is now on display in the London War Museum, instead of commanding its rightful place in the Monaghan Museum.

Although Longford is the sole county which can not claim to have produced a VC award holder, it is one of the few that holds the grave of a recipient. Co. Cork native, *Joseph Ward* of Kinsale, one of the 19 VC's interred in their native land lies at rest in the Church of Ireland graveyard at Longford town.

1916 Fatal Ship Collision at Carlingford Lough

In the pretty little villages which hug the Carlingford Lough coastline, including Killowen, Cranfield and Rostrevor, many inhabitants often reminisce and relive the horrific events visited on their families and neighbours in that idyllic area of Co. Down, on 4th November 1916.

Recently, I was mooching around the ancient St. Bronagh's Monastery, in Rostrevor's Kilbroney graveyard, when I happened upon the burial plot of James Boyle. A symbol chiselled into his headstone caught my eye and whetted my curiosity causing me to delve further. It transpires that in his younger days, James - a native of the nearby hamlet of Killowen - was drawn towards boats, ships and anything that floated on water. At a tender age he went to sea, and 1916 found him aboard the Retriever. This solid ship had already survived a collision when the Spanish Lista went to the bottom of Liverpool Bay. The Retriever was built for the Clanrye Shipping Company of Newry. On the night of 3rd November 1916 it was skippered by the experienced Patrick O'Neill from Kilkeel, with the assistance of his son Joseph. Twenty one year old James Boyle, from Warrenpoint, was their fireman.

The vessel departed Port Garston, on the Mersey, with its cargo of coal intending to arrive in Newry on the following morning. Once out in the open sea, it bore the full brunt of a raging storm. Despite its cargo shifting and slowing her progress, the crew decided that they could ride out the conditions rather than sail back to port, and the Retriever continued to plough the waters of the Irish Sea westward towards the Co. Louth coastline.

Meanwhile, despite the repeated advice from Greenore RIC, the Connemara, built in 1897, had set out on the first leg of her journey from Greenore Port, Co. Louth with the intention of stopping off in Wales and then continuing her voyage to America. Initially her captain hesitated and delayed putting to sea because of the gale force winds. After much pressure and assurances, the captain arranged his crew and set out, around 8pm, on the difficult journey, with 51 concerned passengers aboard. Some had boarded intending to emigrate to the US, while other passengers had arranged to alight on reaching Hollyhead. A large heard of cattle, destined for the British market, was also aboard the powerful Connemara.

At first the journey was uneventful and its passage was afforded sheltered protection from the headlands on either side of Carlingford Lough. However, less than an hour into its journey and on reaching the lighthouse at the mouth of the bay near Cranfield point, the weather deteriorated rapidly. A gale force storm, the worst in living memory, had taken control and pounded all shipping in that area.

This, with high tide and the rising swells at the mouth to the open sea, was creating a perilous situation and unknown to the crew of the Connemara, worse was about to unfold. At the same time on that treacherous night, the Greenore-bound Retriever, was limping its way towards the narrow entrance to Carlingford Bay, and about half a mile away.

Its Captain was guided by the lighthouse between Ballagan Point on the Co. Louth side and Cranfield Point on the Co. Down shoreline. Watching from his vantage position, the light keeper became concerned at the narrowing space between the passing ships. Attempting to alert all to possible danger, he discharged some rocket flares, but his alarm went unheeded and the vessels held their perilous course. While the reason was never established, it seemed as if some unexplained force, combined with the unpredictable swells, took hold of both ships and locked them in fatal combat.

Fireman James Boyle, the only non-swimmer in the crew, was working in the engine room of the Retriever when the collision occurred and he rushed up on deck immediately. Eventually he found himself clinging to an upturned life boat and held tight. Despite being tossed about in the raging sea, James, now barely conscious, found his feet dragging along on a sandy coastal beach. A local farmer, Robert Hanna, who had seen the distress flares, battled through the storm from his home near Cranfield and assisted the exhausted sailor to safety.

When daylight dawned it unveiled a horrific sight of bodies, dead animals and cargo washed up along the Co. Down coastline from Greencastle to Kilkeel. Due to their injuries many of the deceased passengers had become unidentifiable. The Retriever's fireman, James Boyle, was destined to be the sole survivor of both crafts involved. All remaining 96 passengers and animals had perished in the freezing waters of Carlingford Bay and all within a short distance of land.

At a hearing, in Belfast, some months later, James Boyle's evidence was crucial.

He confirmed that from his position aboard the Retriever, at about 9pm, he observed the lights of the approaching Connemara bearing-in and on its correct side but this did not raise any concern to James or his crew. He returned down to his station to replenish the fire and immediately he heard the Retrievers' telegraph ring three times. Now fearing the worst he raced back to deck intending to observe, but then felt the horrific and deadly collision against the Connemara.

Within minutes the Connemara was engulfed in fire and unfortunately the stricken vessel lacked the time to launch any lifeboats before surrendering herself to the towering waves.

Meanwhile Captain O'Neill and the crew aboard the Retriever maintained order, all confident that their ship would ride out the conditions. They launched the lifeboats and started the process of evacuating the ship. Just when it seemed that all souls aboard would be saved, the Retriever rolled over and suctioned all within its reach into the dark watery depths. In his evidence the sole survivor James Boyle confirmed that he was tossed about in the waves for hours, and eventually carried to dry land where he was helped ashore by a local resident. James Boyle enjoyed life for a further 50 years until his natural death in April 1967. He was laid to rest in the historic Kilbroney cemetery, near Rostrevor.

A commemorative headstone also now stands in Kilkeel graveyard to acknowledge and commemorate all the victims of that tragedy, most of whom lie in rest there in Kilkeel, Co. Down.

General Robert Ross

Robert Ross was born in 1766 in a village in Co Down, now called Rostrevor, which bears his name sake.

The Ross family originated in Scotland but socially and politically considered themselves Anglo-Irish. The family was steeped in a history of British military service. David Ross, father of Robert, was himself a distinguished soldier. Robert's mother was a half-sister of the Earl of Charlemont in Co Armagh - one of the leading Irish politicians of the late eighteenth century. His brother and uncle were long-serving members of the Irish Parliament, representing Carlingford and Newry respectively. His father and grandfather also served at one time in the Irish Parliament. So then, it was little surprise that upon graduating from Trinity College Dublin, Robert joined the British Army.

Once in uniform, Robert Ross was sent abroad to protect Britain's interests - to France, Spain, the Netherlands and also Egypt. Known for his bravery, he had many lucky escapes as he led from the front. Because of his exploits he was awarded three Gold Medals and a Sword of Honour from Parliament in recognition. Despite being a strict disciplinarian who was tough on his subordinates, he was well respected by his men as he fought alongside them and shared in the hardship of war. Ross rose through the ranks rapidly and by 1812 had achieved the rank of Major General.

In 1813 the General was appointed to serve under the Duke of Wellington in the Peninsula War and commanded his Regiment at many battles in the same year at Victoria and Roncesvalles. In late 1813 he took a life threatening neck injury at the battle of Orthez, in Spain, but in his usual casual manner he made light of the wound. However when his protective wife, Elizabeth, received word and realised the danger, she rode on horseback through the snow from Bilbao across the Pyrenees and nursed him back to health on the safer French side of the mountain.

No sooner had General Ross returned to work, than he was put in charge of a force bound for the USA. Prior to leaving, he promised his wife that this would be his last expedition and his words proved to be prophetic, but not as he envisaged.

In May of 1884, Earl Bathurst - the British Secretary of State for the colonies - gave Ross his instructions. His company's task was to create a diversion along the border so as to take pressure off other British divisions operating in Canada in trying to repel the American army. Robert Ross was not expected to take possession or annex any ground and instructed not to interfere with the inhabitants or their property. He was however mandated to destroy or remove all US government munitions, harbours and shipping and had license to retaliate if his company came under attack.

On 19 August 1884 Ross and his troops landed near Benedict, Maryland and began their forty mile advance on Washington. Five days later, near Bladensburg, Ross was confronted by a superior number of American soldiers, led by General William Winder, but when opposed, the poorly trained Americans fled in panic. That incident became known as the Bladensburg Races and more disgrace was to follow. The British now seized their advantage and chased the Americans through the streets of Washington and, in panic President Madison and the remainder of the federal administration fled the city.

Ross sent a party under a flag of truce to agree surrender terms, but when it came under attack, the offer was withdrawn. The British immediately set fire to and destroyed the White House and all its connected State buildings.

Although he was reportedly not keen on doing so, in September of that year Ross mounted a raid on Baltimore, then the third largest city in the United States. He landed his troops 16 miles from the city while the Royal Navy attacked Fort Henry, which stood guarding the city harbour. This time the British encountered greater determined American resistance as their Military commanders had made careful preparation, having learned from the Washington debacle. At each attempt the American militia repelled Ross's attempts to penetrate the city. This was the end of Robert Ross's campaign as he was hit by a sniper's bullet which pierced his chest, causing him to die within hours. His body was retrieved and interned at Halifax, Nova Scotia on 29 Sept 1814. Therefore, contrary to his wishes, he never made it back to his beloved Rostrevor.

To mark the death of Captain Ross and the bicentenary of the writing of the American National Anthem and its links to Rostrevor, a Star Spangled Banner Festival was held on Saturday 13 September 2014 in Rostrevor. This included costumed tours of the village and a General Ross exhibition with film about Rostrevor in the Presbyterian Church Hall. A lecture on the events of the 1812–14 War was given by local historian Dr John McCavitt at the Ross Monument on Saturday and Sunday, and live music took place in the village Square. A giant 42 ft x 30ft replica of the original Star Spangled Banner Flag, that flew over Fort McHenry at the end of the 1812-14 War and which coincided with the writing of the American National Anthem by Francis Scot Key in Sept 1814, was unfurled by Rostrevor schoolchildren on that weekend.

The highlight of the event was a spectacular fireworks display and recreation of the bombardment of Fort McHenry at 9pm on the Saturday evening, 13th Sept 2014. From 8.30 pm, the public A2 road between Rostrevor and Warrenpoint was closed to facilitate the event planned alongside the 100ft granite Ross Monument, overlooking Carlingford Lough.

From early on that humid evening, hundreds gathered in the square in Rostrevor and, on signal from the stewards, our group became part of the crowd as we strode out to the Monument. On arrival we were met by hundreds more. They had walked the two miles from Warrenpoint. The huge assembly was treated to a lecture outlining the Robert Ross story and introduced the re-enactment Navy assault – which was about to begin.

At 9pm, the bombardment commenced from a large boat at anchor, within view on the waters of Carlingford Lough. Every few minutes another bomb, emitting coloured smoke and accompanied by a shattering sound, would blast into the darkening sky. This display re-enacting the siege on Fort Mc Henry, in Baltimore, USA by Ross in 1814 where Ross met his death, was an astonishing sight and a glorious education.

China's Great Wall

From an early age I have been intrigued by walls, particularly those constructed from stone. Walls almost as old as the humans who were quick to realise their value and raise them as defences, and to mark out their territory. My direct connection with walls and their stone properties was cultivated growing up on a small stone wall-carved farm where fields, farms and town-lands were defined by these man-made free standing barriers. Our livestock, particularly our athletic sheep, held an inherent view that the next field was always greener and they regularly knocked huge breaches to gain entry across the stone divides. The taller the wall, the greater the challenge and the higher our energetic sheep jumped.

My constant rebuilding provided an insight and respect for that special material. I found that each stone seemed to possess its own persona as no two were alike in shape, size or weight. From the practice of constant rebuilding I acquired an eye for selecting the appropriate stone for each unique space and with the added ingredient of patience, the work of art was completed.

In time I heard of greater walls and became determined to visit each one. The nearest and most accessible was the historic walls of Derry. However when I arrived there in 1971, I found this monument decorated in reams of rusty barbed wire, and by written order, ruled strictly out of bounds. I decided to obey and made a quick departure.

My attention then redirected to another wall, but before time or finance allowed, I was startled to witness, on television, that this robust Berlin wall was being chipped to pieces by chisel-yielding prospectors and dispersed in souvenir form around the world.

Luckily there remained an additional but remote wall, which appeared powerful and permanent and I resolved to conquer this landmark before it too disappeared. Eventually I arrived with my family in the bustling city of Beijing.

The following day at 5 am on a dry Tuesday morning our bus chugged through the city smog. The early start was necessary, as we were aware that our visit and wall climb would need to be completed before the arrival of the scorching mid-day heat. Even an hour later, having negotiated through the mayhem of the milling car and bicycle traffic, the rising heat was becoming very uncomfortable. On that special morning it seemed that most of their 10 million bicycles and 2 million cars were already on the streets travelling in their usual China roulette fashion, showing little regard for traffic lights and none for lane discipline. It was amusing to experience all types of traffic, from pedestrians, rickshaws and cars intermingling in an amazing and apparently dangerous symphony, yet remarkably the place remained accident free.

After travelling for an hour we escaped the traffic madness and left the worst of the thick ever-present smog behind, but the searing temperature continued to increase. At last the outline of the Great Wall appeared snaking along the crest of the mountain in the far distance. Its majestic appearance caused great excitement and banter in our bus and had the effect of making the intense heat bearable.

On arrival at the base we were issued with instructions, tickets and a timetable and then let loose to join the throng of teeming tourists already there. The early part of the climb was difficult, mainly due to the multitude of climbers as they squeezed past one another, competing for the limited room on the 12' wide wall in their inward and outward trek.

As I gained altitude, I found that the heat and steepness tested the less agile, causing the crowds to peter out and fewer bodies provided more space and easier passage. The frequent redundant lookout towers, located at military vantage points, were a Godsend and served as a rest place, a cool box and provided a photo point opportunity. Each tower represented a mental milestone in my quest to claim the summit. As no two steps were of a similar height it was difficult to establish a walking rhythm. However I did reach the summit of my section and was thrilled and felt privileged to stand high up on one of the few man-made structures visible from space. A structure built in 287 BC and restored in 1488, stretching an amazing 1,400 miles in length, and which did not serve its intended purpose of repelling barbarian invasions, as bribery was as rife then as it is now. While some sections of the ancient wall had crumbled I could see the signs of ongoing repairs and learned that the official intention is to restore the entire wall to its former glory. This time, to maintain it as a tourist attraction, rather than for military purpose.

Free Travel Pass

When I heard a shrill voice coming from within the party's noisy crowd with "God Bless Charlie", I wondered who was this great Charlie that was been crowned with Holy accolades. My first thoughts rested on the Scottish Bonny Prince Charlie who was spirited away by the daring Flora McDonald, to take refuge on the Isle of Skye in order to save his life from the Red Coats. Later. when an opportunity arose towards the end of the soirée, I asked the source of this outburst which Charlie she had referred to and the reason for her blessing of him. "It's my free bus pass!", she exclaimed, as if I should have known about this great indulgence all along.

As Minister for Finance in 1968, the wily Charles Haughey TD had introduced the availability of free travel on all public transport, bus and train alike, to all Irish citizens, North and South, on their reaching the golden age of 66. This notion was an astute and targeted political introduction as it endeared him and his political party, to the 'grey voters' - that very dependable section of society which flock to the polling booth in big numbers, at every election.

At that period this novel innovation had little affect on me, other than to cause a hearty laugh. I could not envisage that age ever descending on me; it was too far away in the foggy mists of the distant future. However this impossible 'golden age' did catch up and enveloped me, and with its arrival I dutifully applied for and was presented with, an new free Travel Pass allowing me free public transport for all of Ireland.

Since then, my semi-retired status has allowed me more time to freely travel and ferret around the North and South and investigate parts and people of Ireland that I had missed during my impoverished camping days. During one of my outings I overheard a discussion critically refer to people like me as "joy-riders" and perhaps that observation is a correct analysis. However, during my long full-time working years I paid directly in my travel fares and contributed indirectly through my 'subvention' Income tax, and now its pay-me-back time. When the notion takes me, I travel light from one locality to another like a nomad, by train or bus. I and my wise fellow travellers provide additional and valuable business to the B&B and hospitality industry in towns stretching from Belfast to Dublin, Westport to Bundoran and Tramore to Rostrevor. Far from being just free transport, this blessing from the State also has the effect of distributing finance around the various cities, towns and villages.

Long-live the genial joy-riders armed with a bus-pass in one hand and a wad of spending cash in the other as he and she explores and enriches our awaiting and welcoming countryside.

Limerick You're a Lady

The previous evening I had arrived by train to the city, and walked from the station to my temporary accommodation. Once inside I did as I always do on arrival - I welcomed myself by brewing a comforting cup of tea. Despite the lateness of the day and feeling the effects of rail lag, I wasn't about to allow the remainder of the evening go to loss. I donned my cap and scarf and headed out to explore.

Whenever I visit a new surround I can't wait to acquaint myself with the geography of the area and I find that the best means to explore locally is by shank's mare. I had travelled through this locality many moons ago by car, but that was during the hasty bustle of working life and time didn't allow me to stop or to fully enjoy and absorb the area. Rather I found it a delaying nuisance in having to negotiate its traffic-filled streets. From now on, time would not be my master; rather I would master of time.

Limerick City was gaily displayed by her modern public lighting, one of the remnant gifts from its Year of Culture in 2014. As I wandered along, and gathered my bearings, I heeded the name of each street and their criss-cross formation. It became apparent to me that this was a planned city, as the streets were wide and ran symmetrically and were at right angels to each other. During my evening dander, Limerick came across as a friendly place where pedestrians acknowledged each other, including this new arrival. Drivers were also quick to respond in a genial manner, when a silly slip was made by venturing to cross the street at the wrong place. Despite the stillness of the evening I didn't hear any song or music escaping from the open doors of local pubs. While rugby and hurling flourish, the initial impression was that music and mirth took a back seat here.

Next morning I awoke very early, as is customary for me whenever I find myself in a strange place. However it wasn't early for some hardy workers, who keep the 'wheels' of the city rotating. From my lofty perch I eyed a young jogger flash passed on the footpath who seemed oblivious to all around her. Directly across the street from my hotel my gaze was drawn to two window cleaners preparing for action. Already they had fastened two robust ropes to the top railing of the tall glass building, probably the tallest modern structure in the city, with the ends trailing on the ground below. Each worker donned a harness and attached themselves to the waiting ropes. Now with cleaning accoutrements in hand they abseiled in unison to various levels while carrying out their work on the huge glass facade.

I glanced again to check on her progress, but the jogger was disappearing from view having almost reached the other side of the Shannon Bridge. The volume of traffic was rapidly increasing and beginning to build at the traffic lights, beneath me.

Up the street a Gárda had collared a motorist and judging by the body language, and the exchange of documents, it appeared that the motorist was not compliant and had questions to answer.

Even though it seemed too early for school, mothers - one with a school bag on each shoulder - were taking their children by the hand across the broad road to the safety of the footpath. The youngsters skipped their way without a care. I looked again to find that the two spider-like cleaners were making great progress, manoeuvring over and back, while attached to their strong web. Their polished glass was sparkling now in the slanting rays of an early sun. After breakfast I was ready and keen to begin another day of out dooring.

While crossing the wide Shannon Bridge I was struck by the variety and numbers of wildfowl that inhabit this resplendent waterway. Easing along its west side I arrived at the historic Treaty Stone. This symbolical reminder evoked thoughts of deceit and treachery dating back to the Treaty of October 1691 between the forces of William of Orange and the defeated King James. In keeping with that agreement, many of the Jacobites sailed away from Ireland, mostly to France, for enlistment in the French army. No sooner were these 'Wildgeese' permanently out of sight, than William of Orange repudiated the treaty and proceeded to confiscate large tracts of lands and properties. Having completed my photographic capture of that famed monument, I doddled back across the Shannon, by way of Thomond Bridge.

King John's Castle was the next iconic structure on my list and I found it with little difficulty. For a building constructed as far back as the 13th century and having withstood many murderous attacks it stands very impressive to this day.

From a grey building I moved to a graveyard at St Mary's Cathedral. The script on the aged headstones there depicted many family names which still endure and others that have come to the end of their lineage. To my disappointment the impressive Church itself was locked. However that didn't deter me from visiting other city churches that were open. Apart from whispering a prayer, I always revel in these awesome structures, mostly constructed prior to mechanisation or the availability of weightlifting cranes.

After a long warm and rewarding day I sauntered back towards the railway station, and as I plodded along I mused that 'Limerick you are indeed a Lady' and you have extended your charm to this satisfied visitor.

A Treat in Rostrevor

Having rounded the corner in Warrenpoint I found myself faced with the shimmering waters of Carlingford Bay resplendent in the bright sunshine. Because of its idyllic setting, and squashed between Co. Louth on my right and the Co. Down coastline on my left, I could now well understand why George Bernard Shaw referred to it as *"more beautiful than the bay of Naples"*. As I wheeled along, I could feel the warm welcome sea-breeze ushering me to my next destination only three miles away. Arriving at the square in Rostrevor, I found a comfortable wooden seat to relax on. From my vantage point and directly in front, I could see that iconic and abiding land-mark - the Clough Mór (big stone) sitting precariously near the summit of Sliabh Martin. To my left, the panorama of Sliabh Foy was on clear display.

Closer at hand, my attention was also drawn to the hoard of yellow-coated workers, striding the wooden scaffolding around St Bronagh's Church of Ireland, in their haste to repair its structure, before the onset of winter.

As I watched the bustle of traffic and pedestrians on that busy streetscape, my eye caught groups of student-like ladies going about in groups of four and consulting their notes from time to time. I presumed they were on a treasure hunt. As one group approached me we found ourselves in conversation. They confirmed that they were from a Presbyterian Church group in Belfast and were staying for the next few days in Rostrevor. They explained that one of their challenges was to buy someone a cup of tea or coffee and asked if I would act as their guinea-pig. I was delighted to oblige and within five minutes was the recipient of a cup of savoury coffee.

Almost immediately I had my opportunity to repay the gesture when their leader asked if I was aware of any unique item existing in Rostrevor village that they could record, to assist them to victory in their contest. I gladly obliged. "Did you ever hear of St Bronagh?", I asked, and was answered with a chorus of "no". Then I pointed them to the chapel located a short walk away up the hill. "Go you in there", I advised, "and past the alter you will notice a small alcove. In there, behind protective bars you will see and can touch an ancient priceless bell. This is the century-old long-lost, but rediscovered, St. Bronagh's Bell - or Clog Bán. Make a note of that artefact and it should win the competition for you", I recommended. Meanwhile their competitor groups continued to visually search up and down the street buildings with little success.

*(By Josephine,
née McDonald)*

McDonald's Of Glencoe

They came in a blizzard, we offered them heat
A roof for their heads, dry shoes for their feet
We wined them and dined them, they ate of our meat
And they slept in the house O MacDonald.

After many false starts I resolved to devote additional quality time in researching and recording my family tree, while the senior members of the clan were still alive to tell their tales. Recording details of relatives in the land of the living was time consuming but relatively straightforward. I utilised the usual methods, particularly of interviewing my aunts and uncles. Gathering information on the family roots proved more difficult. In time my initial tree grew into a forest of names, dates, births, marriages and deaths. The overall indication was that my Mc Donald forebears came from outside Ireland and smitten by this knowledge, it became imperative that I embark on an exotic trail.

On completion of the two-hour boat journey, I departed Stranraer and drove North in the direction of the Scottish town of Ayr, where the towering rock formation of Elsa Craig came into view, spiralling directly from its Atlantic blanket, like an enormous rugged fish. Having passed through Inverary, the silhouette of a proud Ben Nevis was visible to my right. This landmark grew bigger and more distinct and guided me as I proceeded towards my destination.

On reaching the outskirts of the highland town of Fort William, I stopped to view a large plinth supporting a life size stone replica of a graceful young woman. On reading the inscription I found it commemorated the daring Flora MacDonald, who assisted Bonny Prince Charlie to escape to the Isle of Skye and as a result suffered arrest and imprisonment in the Tower of London. This was the first indication that the MacDonalds were not always granted sanctuary in their native Scotland.

Later that evening I called to the Tourist Office and seeking advice there, the assistant told me that her name was Campbell and she joked that our families were not always on speaking terms.

Next day I completed my journey by travelling to the tiny and now peaceful village of Glencoe. This silent area had been the stronghold of the MacDonalds, who for centuries lived in harmony with nature and their neighbours, including the prominent Campbell Clan. That was until the English authorities attempted to subdue Scotland and bring that country under the realm of the English Monarch. Even then, the MacDonalds were a stubborn lot and refused to submit to a foreign authority, preferring their simple and independent lifestyle, which they had enjoyed from time immemorial. The Campbells, however, were of a different hue and not alone did they readily submit to English rule but they became willing agents for the foreigners, and were encouraged by their masters to seize and possess MacDonald lands and property.

In August 1691, a Royal Proclamation was issued requiring all highland chiefs to take the oath of allegiance, to the Crown, before 1st January 1692, and threatening those who refused with fire and sword. The proclamation had the desired effect with most of their chiefs swearing loyalty. However, it was not in the nature of MacDonalds to fall to subserviency and their leadership were slow to succumb. On 31 December 1691, the MacDonald Chief went to Fort William but no English officer was present to administer the oath. Realising the imminent danger, MacDonald and his company set off through the snow to Inverary but again his adversary - Sir Colin Campbell - was not there as promised to accept the oath. After a forced wait of three days in the freezing winter MacDonald eventually managed to take the oath, but the delay was interpreted as an act of disobedience, so MacDonald became a wanted man.

On 7th January 1692 a party of Mounted Argyles led by Captain Campbell, arrived at Glencoe with murder in mind. The unsuspecting and affable MacDonalds widened the circle and entertained the Campbell visitors with stories, song and food before all retired for the night. But as pre-arranged, in the early hours of the morning, Campbell and his soldiers set about their bloody business of murder and arson. Many of the young MacDonalds were put to the sword, while the older members were turned out into the night to die of exposure in the bitter snow-covered mountains in one of Scotland's harshest winters. Some of the clan did succeed in escaping through the mountains and on to the relative safety of Ulster.

While I failed to unearth documented evidence, the likelihood is, that through my forebears I am historically linked with Glencoe and sometimes I can feel it in my bones.

Oh, cruel is the snow that sweeps Glencoe
And covers the grave of MacDonald
Oh, cruel is the foe that raids Glencoe
And murders the house O MacDonald.

A Doll of Grace

On the 14 September 1982 it was announced to the world that Princess Grace had died, at the early age of 52. She had been driving through France on her return to her Principality of Monaco when disaster struck. Her vehicle careened off the highway into a deep ravine and her daughter Caroline, lucky to survive the impact, crawled back up the steep embankment to raise the alarm.

Born Grace Patricia in Philadelphia to John and Margaret Kelly, in November 1929; she was one of four children. Her father was the son of an Irish emigrant from Westport, Co Mayo, while her mother hailed from Germany. From an early age, Grace exhibited a restless and spirited outlook.

In her teens she leaned towards acting and, blessed with beauty and poise, she soon attracted notice from high profile film-makers. As a result she was cast in 'High Noon' after being spotted for her acting off Broadway.

In New York, her natural beauty was in high demand for advertisements and modelling. Occasionally, her radiant face shone out from high profile magazine covers such as Cosmopolitan.

After moving to Hollywood she proved that she was more than just a pretty face and her unique acting ability was acknowledged through starring roles in numerous films, and eventually winning an Oscar for her performance in *"The Country Girl"*.

In 1956, she married Prince Rainier and became Her Highness Princess Grace of Monaco and due to her royal status she was obliged to forgo her successful acting career. She had three children – Caroline, Albert and Stephanie.

Because of her nostalgic attachment to Ireland, Prince Rainier and Princess Grace purchased her ancestral home - a cottage on a 35-acre farm near Newport Village, Co Mayo, where her grandfather lived before emigrating to the United States.

While I take a passing interest in fashion trends and renowned personalities, I maintain a special admiration for Princess Grace because of her private generosity to me.

For whatever reason, my ingenious mother, in the late 50's and without my knowledge, sent my scribbled birthday request to Princess Grace at her Palace in Monaco, hoping that the Princess would act as a fairy godmother to me. Princess Grace, despite all her important royal and family commitments, didn't disappoint.

She responded by posting a beautiful doll addressed to me, complete with palace stamp, to my address in Co Monaghan, an area with which she had no connection. Her timing was perfect as a most exquisite doll, arrived at my home just in time for my birthday.

This was no ordinary doll, she wore a lovely long flowing lace dress and matching bonnet, which framed a head of gold curling hair, and her little cute face was picture-perfect. Her outfit was complete with blue ribbons, lace petticoat, shoes, socks and pants – all trimmed with lace.

Now many years later I still treasure this doll, which I have kept in pristine condition. I preserve it in its original box, complete with postal confirmation and original wrapping paper. Some day I will pass this treasure, along with its magical story, to my daughter as a family heirloom.

My only regret is that I don't have a copy of the correspondence which passed between my late mother and Princess Grace. The occasional mention of the Princess and her life, brings my doll and her generosity to an unknown child waiting for a surprise, into pleasant focus.

Each time I look at my special doll I think in admiration of the foresight of my mother who, on the off-chance, sent my childish letter to a celebrity and I was rewarded by a beautiful gift from a special Princess.

Better Late And Alive

Every year my three friends and I saved a little each week from our meagre wages as clerks with Monaghan County Council which enabled us book our annual week's holiday in distant Ballybunion, Tramore or Bundoran. However, when our incomes improved we decided to put by a little extra each week, in preparation for the big one.

Armed with suitcases of summer clothes and beach wear we set off by bus to the North Wall in Dublin and boarded a boat there, which ferried us to Douglas on the Isle of Man – the next best place to Spain.

It was our first holiday abroad and the year was 1973. For the first four days the accommodation and weather were beautiful. Each day we lazed about and bathed on the sun-drenched beach of Douglas. In the cool of the evenings we walked the packed promenade and later climbed the hills. Most nights we finished off our day's entertainment in the world's largest indoor holiday resort - known as Summerland - to enjoy the cabaret.

On the evening of 2nd August my friends were proving difficult to rouse from their siesta, after a busy afternoon of walking and sightseeing, and so while waiting for them to arise from their slumber I decided on a short walk. Once outside, my attention was drawn to the continuous noise of ambulance and fire brigade sirens and I decided to investigate what was causing the commotion. As I headed out on the 15 minute walk along the beach, I experienced an unusual and putrid smell in the air. As I came within view of Summerland, I saw a huge fireball and thick black smoke bellowing skyward from our venue of nightly entertainment, which had now become a fireball pouring crimson angry flames towering into a grey sky.

This particular evening, the exceptional chilling breeze had driven nearly 3,000 holiday-makers into the warmth of that centre. At this stage the fire brigades and ambulances, with roaring sirens, were screeching along the promenade, and watching in fear and disbelief I saw hoards of Summerland patrons tumble out at various points, many of whom were visibly suffering from shock and injury and in a state of total confusion.

Men, women and children were crying out for their loved ones still trapped within the walls of liquid fire, in the horrifying inferno. Despite the heroic work of the emergency services, many holiday-makers were to die from smoke inhalation, more as a result of burns from the boiling, dripping, melting plastic, while others perished from being trampled on by panicking patrons in their furious stampede in attempting to escape the tragedy.

The unfortunate bingo players who held their session in the basement were the last to become aware of the unfolding tragedy and had little or no hope of escape from the catastrophe, with their lives.

Emergency vehicles raced up and down the promenade advising and providing instructions through loudhailers. The announcers also implored members of the public to come forward immediately as blood donors.

Summerland was built in 1971 as Britain's first forget-the-weather family fun centre, at a cost of two million pounds. Douglas Council was so eager that they waived some local by-laws to accommodate its speedy construction. The complex boasted many sections and levels, from basement bingo halls to upstairs live cabaret shows and amusement arcades. The construction materials, though considered adequate at the time, were not fire proofed and in the event its extensive plastic dome proved extremely combustible.

As the seating was not allocated and therefore filled from floor level upwards, those patrons who arrived last found that they would be relegated to the seating high up in the 96ft tall building. This state of art complex was enclosed within an enormous transparent and robust flammable plastic dome.

On that fateful evening in 1973, just two years after Summerland was opened for business, the lucrative dream became a nightmare and cost fifty people their lives, ten of whom were children.

As I stood watching the horrific spectacle from a safe distance the thought struck me that had my companions and I set out at our normal departure time, we too would now be seated high up on our usual perch, which had now become death row within that devouring fire.

In that early 70's period the electronic contact between Ireland and the Isle of Man was antiquated and as a result of the fire, the limited phone lines that did exist and continued to function, were jammed for days making cross-channel communication impossible. So I was unable to make contact with home to reassure my relatives in Monaghan for the first two days.

On my safe arrival back home I received a hero's welcome from my relieved family.

Flora McDonald

When I received the unexpected invitation from my friends in Middletown to join their Scottish outing, I dropped everything and agreed, particularly when a visit to Glencoe was part of the agenda. Setting out on our excursion from Armagh, the warm sun shone and continued to follow us on all five days. After the crossing from Belfast to Cairnryan we boarded again and motored towards our Lough Lomond Hotel.

Next morning brought an early rise as a long day stretched ahead of us and all 40 were ushered into a boat and enjoyed the unique privilege of floating across the storied waters of Loch Lomond, to reach our waiting coach on the opposite bank. On board again, we were heading for Glencoe, former stronghold of the MacDonald Clan until that fateful winter night on 7th January 1692 when most were slain by their neighbouring Campbell overlords, in a planned attack of blatant butchery.

On reaching that scenic and rugged area I could sense the horror and feel the lingering aura of sadness haunting this locality. Maybe this is because I am a MacDonald myself, and could well be a descendant from one of the few who escaped to Ulster and so avoided death on that horrific night.

Some miles further, just outside Forth William, I paid a visit to the life-size statue of the famous Flora Mc Donald. Indeed, she could be my distant relative. Flora was born, in a small island in the Outer Hebrides in 1722 into a Presbyterian family. Shortly after her birth her father died and her mother married again, this time to a man on the Scottish mainland. Flora's stepfather, Hugh MacDonald - a renowned swordsman - had served in the French army, and was now commander of the local militia.

In 1746 political turmoil was poisoning the Scottish air, but despite holding great promise, the pending Battle of Culloden turned out to be a disaster for the Jacobites including their leader, Prince Charles Stuart, better known as Bonnie Prince Charlie. Immediately afterwards, the Act of Proscription was enacted with the purpose of destroying Scottish culture, including the use of their traditional dress. The Act was to remain in force until 1782

Now a fugitive with a huge price on his head, it was a case of escape to freedom or submission to immediate death, for the Prince. Despite her tender age of 24 years, the spirited Flora Mc Donald was prevailed on to assist in finding a means of escape to temporary safety onto the Isle of Skye. To obtain a pass and a boat she had to confide in and enlist the help of her military stepfather. Despite the dire consequences if his involvement was detected, he agreed to assist on the pretence that Flora was going to visit her mother, who was then living on that Isle.

On the night of 27/28 June 1746, along with six Jacobite oarsmen, the daring Flora boarded a boat in the company of her 'Irish maid' Betty Burke, dressed in Irish costume and all headed out from Benbecula Bay. After much evasive manoeuvring over the dark waters, to avoid the attentions of the Redcoats, Flora's party landed safely and unobserved on the hallowed soil of Skye. In order to become invisible, the party split up and 'Betty Burke' made it to a safe house awaiting the arrival of Bonnie Prince Charlie. Within a week, now attired in normal dress, his friends assisted the Prince in stowing away to France.

Meanwhile back on the mainland the searching authorities had noted Flora's absence and on her return she was arrested and questioned, by the Redcoats, about her 'Betty Bourke' passenger. The young maiden was taken under armed guard, the long and difficult journey to the Tower of London. While she languished there in miserable captive conditions awaiting her fate. Her influential stepfather, while fearing the worst, was busy making representations to win her freedom.

Luckily for Flora one year later in 1747, King George announced an amnesty and she was among those set free. She immediately made her way back the long journey to her beloved Scotland again.

In 1750, at the age of 28, Flora married Alan MacDonald and over the years they had seven children. During their early years of marriage they enjoyed financial success, but hard times were about to knock. So once again Flora, with her family, found herself back on the Isle of Skye as her husband's roots lay there.

In 1774 Flora and her family sailed to North Carolina to start a new life as plantation owners. No sooner had they settled when they were visited by political upheaval once again. This time it was the American War of Independence. Because her husband had military expertise he was conscripted on the side of the British Redcoats. However he saw little fighting as he was captured early and imprisoned by the foe.

While imprisoned, their plantation was destroyed and property stolen and on his release in 1778 Alan followed his family who had fled to the safety of Canada. As life there was harsh and unprofitable the family decided to abandon Canada and return to their native Isle of Skye.

The adventurous Flora Mc Donald, immortalised by the Skye Boat song, died in March 1790 at the age of 68 and lies at rest in Kilmuir cemetery. Despite its remoteness, her resting place, marked by a high Celtic cross on the Isle of Skye, continues to be one of the most visited graves in all of Scotland.

Monastic Settlements of Rostrevor

Within the last 20 years, a Monastery founded by the Benedictine Order of France has been built in Rostrevor. In 1998, five Monks from Bec in Normandy came to Rostrevor on invitation from the Irish Catholic hierarchy, in search of a site where they could build their Irish Headquarters and settle down to prayer and work in assisting with the peace process. On arrival to that Co. Down village they set up temporary home in the old former Convent in Rostrevor village. Having spent some two years there making contacts and enquires, the monks met with little success in finding a suitable site on which to lay their foundation. Having given up hope of founding their intended new Monastery they decided to arrange a farewell event prior to departure, in October 2000. Miraculously, nearing the end of this final public prayer meeting, their superior was approached by a local farming couple. This elderly childless pair, Paddy Joe Kielty and his wife Philomena, nee McDonald, offered to donate half of their small farm, lying two miles from Rostrevor in the nearby Kilbroney valley, to the Monks. The Benedictines discussed this generous offer but, due to its inadequate size, reluctantly told the couple that they were unable to accept their kind gesture and therefore would be departing Ireland and returning home to France permanently. A short time later that couple returned and further shocked the monks by advising that they would be happy to donate their full holding. The monks were delighted to immediately accept their generous donation and complete the legal transfer of ownership. Work started on the project in 2002 and completed in 2004. Holy Cross Monastery was officially opened for worship on 18 January 2004 in an ecumenical prayer service involving representatives from all the main Churches in Ireland.

The farming husband and wife who donated the land have since passed away and, in keeping with their wishes, are now buried on the Monastery grounds. Their headstone relates the unique story.

Holy Cross was to become the first new Monastery to open its doors in Ireland or the UK in the last 800 years. This rare occurrence is a case of history repeating itself, as approximately one mile further back, nearer to Rostrevor village in the same Kilbroney Valley, the remnants of a 6th Century Monastery, founded by St Bronagh is visible to this day. She is also reputed to have arrived from France and her tall granite cross and holy well are located in the much-visited and peaceful valley within Kilbroney graveyard. Bronagh, or Bróna, is the Patron Saint of seafarers She and her order may have found their way to

Co. Down by default as victims of one of the many shipwreck incidences in the nearby waters of Carlingford Lough.

When I first heard about St. Bronagh, curiosity caused me to delve further and my research led me to believe that the name Bronagh or Bróna is uniquely related to Co. Down. So, to learn more I took to the road and travelled northwards, arriving in Rostrevor. This settlement, bigger than a village, yet too small to claim township, enjoys an elevated setting overlooking Carlingford Bay and nestles gently within the protection of the Mourne Mountains.

Now all historians will agree that a good starting point to acquire a feel and knowledge of a district and its people, is within its graveyard. During my excursion and having ventured out the Hilltown Road, I arrived at an ancient burial ground. Opening its heavy iron gate I entered Kilbroney Cemetery. There in the valley I sensed that this area was not alone unique in its idyllic setting, but also in its serenity.

Amongst the many interesting head stones my attention was drawn to a tall cross and on reading the inscription I found it to commemorate the Giant Murphy, a native of the nearby Killowen hamlet, who during his short lifetime from 1834 to 1862, at 8'1" was then the tallest person in the world. Further along I noticed a substantial granite headstone erected in memory of St Bronagh. In the background a roofless stone building stood, which in its day, served as the Church of St. Bronagh. On inquiring, I learned that in the 6th century AD Bronagh was a nun who arrived from Normandy by boat, making land at nearby Warrenpoint.

With her small community of nuns she received a warm welcome from the friendly people of Rostrevor who provided her with a plot of land near the village. There she became self sufficient, built her Church and from her small Convent served her adopted fold. While many monastic settlements were equipped with a bell or a crosier, Bronagh's shrine was uniquely in possession of both symbols. Sadly her crosier went missing in the 15th century but St. Bronagh's bell unearths a wonderful true story.

During its active service the Kilbroney Bell or "Clogh Bán" was secured between the branches of a young oak tree, beside her Monastery, and chimed at intervals to signal the frequent call to prayer. Due to the passing of time and occasional attacks, the Convent and its nuns faded away and the symbolic bell was forgotten and disappeared. However country people insisted that, on their journey to and from Rostrevor on windy nights, they could hear the ghostly peal of a bell as they walked passed what had become the Catholic graveyard, and, gripped with fear they quickened their step as they prayed for the Holy Souls. Many travellers interpreted the sound as a warning of a sudden or imminent death within their community.

On a night in 1885 when a fierce storm raged across Ireland, Rostrevor was not spared. The morning following the 'Night of the Big Wind' the mystery of Bronagh's missing bell was solved. A casualty amongst the fallen debris was a giant oak tree beside St Bronagh's former Monastery. Now in the throes of death the ancient oak was about to unfold its incredible long-held secret, which had puzzled generations of Rostrevor folk. In falling, a branch had severed from the tree revealing a cavity within the trunk, and safe inside the cavern nestled St Bronagh's missing bell, perfectly preserved in pristine condition.

The coveted discovery was taken to Newry for use in the Old Chapel and later housed in Newry Convent. That was until the sharp-eyed Parish Priest of Rostrevor, Rev. Patrick O'Neill, having observed and identified the Bell, promptly conveyed it back to Kilbroney.

Today this bell can be viewed and chimed at its secure and permanent home, on display in Rostrevor Chapel, where, in keeping with local tradition, I made my wish and sounded it on my visit there. It is said that the first time the recovered bell was used it brought tears to the eyes of many worshippers.

While Bronagh, the Patron Saint of seafarers, has long since departed, her presence and influence continues around Rostrevor as her name is embedded in its environment and culture. Housing developments, the local Church of Ireland, the amenity park and the local GAA are but a few institutions that bear her name. Bronagh remains a popular name for girls in that area of south Co Down and across Ulster. Saint Bronagh's bell, on permanent display, confirms that it will endure as a tangible testament to that Saint's place in time and her ministry at Rostrevor.

Saint Bronagh's annual feast day is celebrated on 2nd of April.

Finvola, the Gem of the Roe

"In the land of O'Cahain where bleak mountains rise
O'er whose brown ridgy tops now the dusky clouds fly
Deep sunk in the valley a wild flower did grow
And her name was Finvola, the Gem of the Roe."

I headed off northwards to fill my head with Irish music and song, but instead I returned home humming a beautiful tune in the English language, marking the memory of an unfortunate young lady of that local area.

Thanks to my musical daughter I became interested in attending na Fleadhanna Ceoil as she was involved in that scene since her childhood. So now whenever I'm free I set out for that weekend, with my family, to absorb the Fleadh Ceoil and enjoy the outdoor music, while taking the opportunity to investigate a new locality. On the occasion when word came that the Ulster Fleadh was bound for Dungiven in Co. Derry, I knew that I could not let this opportunity escape as it was one of the few areas in Ireland that I had never visited. However, I was aware that this landscape, packed with myth and legends, has a historical association with the Scottish MacDonald clan, who are reputed to be linked to *my* branch of the same MacDonald tribe.

On my journey northwards from Monaghan I decided to travel along the left-hand side of Lough Neagh. This scenic route gave me sight of that renowned waterway and its islands. I stopped at Ardboe point to relax and while seated at the idyllic picnic area I ate a bite of lunch while the crystal cool waters lapped around, soothing my bare feet. Well rested, I twisted the key and set out again. Another twenty miles and I found myself emerging onto the A6 motorway. The finger-post there announced that Belfast was on my right and Derry was to my left. As I wheeled to the left I found that I was now driving along the Glenshane Pass. This rugged landscape was familiar to me only through the weather forecasts depicted on television; particularly when the annual winter snow-drifts bring this elevated and stunning valley to a stand-still. On this fine summer day, and shortly after motoring past Ulster's most elevated pub, I arrived in the pretty town of Dungiven.

As the passing traffic had been diverted away from the town centre, the spacious streets provided an ideal arena to accommodate the wandering crowds and the array of splendid musicians. While dodging about, my eye caught an ancient castle-like building standing just off the Main St., it tempted me to investigate further.

Reading the information from the small official wall plaque I learned that this was the Old Priory which, in its day, was the place of worship used by the ruling O'Cathain Family. For generations they had governed the lands around Dungiven from their nearby fortified Castle overlooking the Roe valley and the River Roe.

Despite being dispossessed during the Ulster plantation, the presence of this Gaelic Chieftain remains evident to this day, as members of that dynasty lie interned in the nearby cemetery. One of their plots holds the grave of the young Finvola O'Cathain-McDonald. Inquiring further I found that there had existed a tradition of trade, merriment and inter-marriage between the local O'Cathain clan and that of the MacDonalds from the Scottish isles.

On one of their frequent social visits to Scotland the vivacious Finvola, daughter of Dermot O'Cathain, met and fell in love with Angus MacDonald, son of Laird MacDonald from the Isle of Islay.

The young couple decided to marry but before the ceremony took place they agreed that in the event of Finvola dying prior to her parents, she would be taken back to Co. Derry for burial in her native Dungiven. This Irish arrangement was in keeping with the O'Cathain custom.

Legend has it that only after a few short years into their marriage the Banshee was heard crying across the Roe valley and this signal alerted O'Cahain that a member of the family had died. Together with his son, the Chieftain sailed for Islay and sure enough was met with the sad news that his beloved daughter, Finvola, had contracted fever and died. When all were agreed that the Irish custom should be honoured, they placed her body in their fishing boat and ferried her back to her Dungiven birthplace. The bereft family laid their daughter in the prepared plot within the quite shadow of the Priory, where Finvola rests to this day. However the Local Authorities have ensured that her memory will survive in Dungiven as she now takes pride-of-place, in artistic form, on Main Street, holding her ornate Harp, for all to see. Also the poignant lament, *"The Gem of the Roe"* was written to celebrate her short life and preserve her in youthful memory through song and story.

"The Gem of the Roe.
The Gem of the Roe,
But gone is Finvola the Gem of the Roe."

Paris and it's Pere Lachaise Cemetery

No doubt the expression "see Rome and die" has merit. However my experience of choice is "enjoy Paris and live".

It all happened with very little warning. Our student daughter wished to test her French on the Parisians in their own environment so she searched out a cheap flight on the internet. My only input was to provide my laser card and she completed the family booking.

We arrived on the wrong side of town but after an hour's learning curve on the unfamiliar Metro we eventually emerged directly outside our comfortable accommodation. After disposing of our cumbersome luggage and a quick meal, we set out to take the city.

By the time we reached our first target it was dark and having hauled ourselves up its one hundred and eighty foot-worn stone steps we reached the top of the Arc de Triumph. Our climb was rewarded by spectacular views from its summit. We were now standing on a huge elevated hub with traffic-filled roads far below, spoking out all around. From our lofty perch we commanded an illuminated aerial view of the city's land marks which we had earmarked for visiting in the coming days.

We kept our second day free to investigate at ground level and emerged from the first Metro ride of the day, directly opposite a continuous high wall. On entering the enclosure through an ancient black gate we found ourselves in Pere Lachaise Cemetery.

In the distance, an elaborate monument caught my attention. On inspection I found it commemorated a 'McDonald' family. The headstone left no doubt that this family was of wealthy stock and I was surprised to note that a family of that name was buried near the centre of Paris. This made me wonder why and when did my branch of the McDonald clan fall off the gravy train.

Another tenuous Monaghan connection was that of the Wilde Family. While his two tragic half sisters - Mary and Emily - lie at rest in the stony grey soil, Oscar Wilde's Paris tomb, judging by its plethora of affectionate lipstick graffiti, must be one of the most revered and frequently visited tombs in the Pere Lachaise Cemetery, spread over its one hundred and eighteen acres.

As we sauntered along we saw a crowd gathered beside a tall marble obelisk engraved with the names of 135 French citizens who had lost their lives in the Egyptian Air crash on 3rd January 2004. We stood in sympathy with the group of relatives there, to commemorate the anniversary of that tragedy.

Amongst the many world-renowned personalities who repose in the Pere Lachaise Cemetery, the resting place of Edith Piaf caught my eye. Born Edith Giovanna Gassion in December 1915, to a seventeen-year old Italian mother and a street acrobat French father, Edith was abandoned as a child and left in the care of her grandmother. Her formative years were spent on the undesirable and wayward side of life, resulting in the neglect of her education.

From the age of three to seven, Edith suffered a period of blindness, but after attending a pilgrimage honouring Saint Therese, her sight was restored. Later she overcame a bout of deafness. At fourteen she joined her father as a street performer, but eventually disagreement set in and she went her own way.

In 1935 her unique singing quality was discovered and exploited by a night club owner. Because of her petite height of 4' 8" she became known in France as *"Mome Piaf"* and around the world as *"The Little Sparrow"*.

During World War II she sang in Paris to the high-ranking occupying German troops. She also entertained the Prisoners of War and assisted the Resistance in their escape plans.

Following the war, she toured across Europe and America and became an international star and performed to capacity audiences in Carnegie Hall.

Sadly, as a result of a serious car accident she developed an addiction to drugs which bedevilled her for the remainder of her short life.

Her first marriage in 1952 lasted for only four years. However, in 1962 Edith married a singer 26 years her junior who was devoted to her until her death the following year.

In October 1963, at the young age of 48, her turbulent life came to an end. On her death, Edith Pief had become one of France's most loved entertainers and it's national icon. She now rests in peace among her famous contemporaries in Pere Lachaise Cemetery.

ॐ

Oscar Wilde and his County Monaghan Connection

As it is well documented, not alone was Oscar Wilde one of Ireland's foremost playwrights, he was also a world-renowned genius. Born in 1854 to an artistic family, Oscar endeared himself to his peers through his exceptional wit and intelligence. While he did experience the good life, his personal life for the most part, was unhappy. His personal orientation set him apart, particularly during a period when homosexuality was deemed a criminal offence. Oscar, during his exile in London, had the added misfortune of becoming romantically involved with Lord Alfred, the son of the Marcus of Queensbury. Because of that liaison, a trial ensued and the outcome resulted in a three-year jail sentence for Oscar Wilde, including hard labour. This captive experience was the catalyst which produced his famous "Ballad of Reading Jail".

In 1897, Wilde emerged from prison as a broken man. The gallery of former admirers which had sustained him, had now deserted; some through disgust, others through fear of association. In 1900, three years after release he died a pauper in Paris and is interred there in the Pere Lachaise cemetery

Oscar Wilde's sufferings also connected him, through a tragic family event, to a quiet corner of Co. Monaghan.

A stiff autumn breeze searched the quiet countryside as a carpet of rustic leaves cushioned the rutted lane-way. A silent procession walked behind the horse-drawn hearse. All dressed immaculately in black with top hats adorning the men folk. Having travelled less than a mile, the small group of mourners reached their destination and halted outside the graveyard. Four robust men stepped forward, lifted the coffin and shouldered it through the narrow gateway to a freshly dug grave. One distinguished looking man stood aside in silent grief as the remains were lowered and the stony soil restored over the coffin. After his daughter Mary was buried, Dr. Wilde walked slowly away from the cemetery.

Three weeks later an exact and poignant sequence was repeated as a similar cortège made its way from The Manor at Drummaconor – the short distance to St. Moha's Church of Ireland cemetery at Drumsnatt Threemilehouse. Once again, Dr Wilde – an eminent eye and ear surgeon from Dublin - stood silent as his second daughter was interred beside her sister. Both girls, Mary aged 22 years and Emily 24 years, had come as guests to visit their cousin, Rev Ralph Wilde, intending to explore and enjoy nearby Monaghan town.

On the night of 31 October 1871 the local gentry decided to hold one of their regular balls and probably because of the presence of the two vivacious sisters, Drummaconnor House was chosen as the venue so as to make their acquaintance with the new city arrivals. This period two-story dwelling, with its imposing steps leading to the front door, boasting ten rooms along with its elegant dining and living room areas, was the ideal setting.

By all accounts the evening was successful and lived beyond expectations. Many of the guests had departed in their carriages and the merriment was winding down when young Mary was persuaded by her host to rise for a last dance. She whirled gaily around in her flowing pleated dress, while enjoying the magic of the moment, but as she glided past the open fire, oblivious to her surroundings, her clothing came in contact with the blazing embers and within seconds she was engulfed in a mass of fire. Her watching sister Emily, aware of the imminent danger, came to Mary's aid but was unable to quell the flames. Mary was bundled downstairs to the cold outdoors but despite being rolled on the wet grass the fireball that encased her continued to burn to such an extent that she died within three days, on 3rd November 1871.

Meanwhile Emily, in attempting to save Mary also became smothered in flames and suffered severe burns. She lingered as an invalid in great pain, and despite the best medical attention available she survived only a further three weeks and was buried alongside her sister in the Church of Ireland Graveyard.

On my visit to Drumsnatt cemetery near the village of Threemilehouse, Co Monaghan, I observed a granite headstone which commemorates Oscar Wilde's half sisters, on which the faded inscription reads – *"In memory of two loving and beloved sisters, Emily Wilde aged 24 years and Mary Wilde aged 22 years, who lost their lives by accident in this Parish in November 1871."*